Residential
Water Demand
and
Economic Development

UNIVERSITY OF TORONTO DEPARTMENT OF GEOGRAPHY RESEARCH PUBLICATIONS

Residential
Water Demand
and
Economic Development

TERENCE R. LEE

Published for the University of Toronto Department of
Geography by the University of Toronto Press

© University of Toronto Department of Geography
Published by University of Toronto Press, 1969
Reprinted 2017
ISBN 978-0-8020-3245-4 (cloth)
ISBN 978-1-4875-8715-4 (paper)

ACKNOWLEDGEMENTS

This study was supported by a fellowship from the International Institute of Education which made it possible for me to spend almost two years in India. Many thanks are due to Jack Robin and all the members of the Ford Foundation Advisory Planning Group to the Calcutta Metropolitan Planning Organization for encouragement, support, and advice while in Calcutta.

The field work for the Bustee study was conducted with the cooperation of Dr. Dilip Pal and his team of field interviewers from the Calcutta Metropolitan Planning Organization. Sukendru Mukherjee and Prem Sharma translated the Kalyani and New Delhi questionnaires into Bengali and Hindi, respectively.

Officials of the World Health Organization, the World Bank, the Pan-American Health Organization and the Agency for International Development provided a great deal of the information concerning urban water supplies in the underdeveloped countries.

Bruce McDougall gave advice and assistance on the multiple correlation analysis.

Ian Burton supported and encouraged the study at all stages from conception to publication; his comments were a continual source of stimulation.

In the later stages of the preparation and publication of the study, the Policy and Planning Branch, Department of Energy, Mines and Resources generously gave me time and assistance.

Comments on drafts of this study were made by Arthur Holloway, Charles Pineo, Derrick Sewell, Harold Shipman, Gilbert White, and Shue Tuck Wong. All the remaining inadequacies and failings are the author's own.

T. R. Lee
Ottawa
March, 1969

CONTENTS

LIST OF TABLES

LIST OF ILLUSTRATIONS

FIGURE

RESIDENTIAL WATER DEMAND
AND ECONOMIC DEVELOPMENT

CHAPTER I

THE PROVISION OF RESIDENTIAL WATER SUPPLIES IN DEVELOPING COUNTRIES

The problem of economic development or progress in the so-
called underdeveloped countries is mainly one of the elemen-
tary removal of hunger, exposure, and disease. Water, as a
resource, has been accepted as a major contributor to the elimination of hunger through irrigation, and the elimination of disease through public water supplies. Unsafe water may be
significant to the high rate of occurrence of disease typical of
the underdeveloped country but, of itself, public water supply
is not a determinant of economic and social progress. It is
part of the necessary social infrastructure needed to support
industrial growth and concomitant urbanization, but the level
of need for public water supplies is by no means securely established.

In the underdeveloped countries, the rapid urban growth of
the last twenty years has generally occurred without a comparable expansion of utilities, including water supply. Growing
disparities between the effective supply of, and demand for,
water have reached very serious proportions and constitute a
possible danger to public health, a danger which is not restricted to the underdeveloped countries themselves. There
has been a growing international concern with these deficiencies in the supply of water and efforts are under way to combat
them at considerable cost. These costs promise to be so high
that careful scrutiny of the expenditures is required and well-
founded justification of the expenditures necessary. The concern with the need for improved water supplies has highlighted
a hiatus in our knowledge of the relationships between water
supply needs and different levels of economic development.

Outside the developed countries a reliable and safe water
supply is a rare occurrence. Public water supply can seldom
be considered "adequate" and the burden of waterborne disease

3

is high. It has been estimated that over 500 million people a year in underdeveloped countries suffer from diseases that can be traced to the use of unsafe water supplies.[1] The high incidence of disease severely strains already overtaxed public health services and adds considerably to the inefficiency of the labour force through loss of time and general debility.

External assistance has been given for the construction of urban water supply, but paradoxically, despite the obvious need for improved water supplies, little attempt has been made to define this need in terms of the contribution of water supply to economic development. Investment decisions have been based on a variety of considerations with an emphasis on the ability to pay.

This study attempts to fill the hiatus in our knowledge of the relationship between water supply and economic development and the components of the demand function for domestic water supply, by examination of the existing water-use system in two urban areas in India.

A basic assumption of the study is that the use of water can be understood as a response to the environment in which the consumer lives. The demand for water shows a systematic variation conditioned by a number of factors in the living environment —a relationship not dependent upon the price of water. It is further assumed that the influence of low income levels and the associated poor living environment is such as to produce a considerable inelasticity in the demand for water. Improvements in the living environment would produce discrete changes in the demand function for water.

The factors significant in influencing water use and consumption are hypothesized as (1) the distance the consumer has to travel to the water source or the availability of water, (2) income, (3) education, (4) religion, and (5) housing. Differences in the availability of water divide the population into two groups: (1) those households with a water connection inside their houses, and (2) households dependent upon public water sources outside the house.

---

[1]John Logan, "The International Municipal Water Supply Program: A Health and Economic Appraisal," American Journal of Tropical Medicine and Hygiene, IX, No. 5 (September, 1960), 470.

It is within these two groups that the factors delineated above are important. The chosen variables are susceptible to quantitative analysis and can be used as indicators of the level of living and its related impact on the level of water consumption. This permits us to specify the nature of the patterns of water consumption that might be expected at different levels of economic development and associated levels of living. This knowledge can help in the formulation of guide lines and provides a method by which estimates of the future levels of water consumption may be improved. It can illuminate the nature of the relationship between (a) water consumption and use, and (b) the price of water and variations in the living environment.

To provide the perspective within which these studies have been made, this chapter first describes one not untypical if rather extreme existing situation, in the city of Calcutta. Then follows a discussion of the search for a policy and rationale for the provision of water supply that has been made by institutions and agencies concerned with the furthering of economic and social development.

Chapter ii develops the specific background to the empirical studies, particularly concerning the nature of the city in India and the relevance of urban structure to the provision of water supply systems. The empirical data discussed in chapters iii and iv are concerned with the relationship between household characteristics and the level of water consumption under a number of differing conditions. The differences observed in water consumption between households are such as to allow for general conclusions to be made about the nature of the demand for domestic water supply with the progress of development.

The contemporary situation in Calcutta is discussed in some detail to provide an illustration of the nature of the problem existing in many cities. The kind of deficiencies and the severity of the problem vary from country to country and city to city. Calcutta can be taken, however, as an example to demonstrate the problems encountered in the provision of water supply and also to establish the severity of the existing deficiencies.

Calcutta's Water Supply
Calcutta has had a filtered water supply system for a relatively long time. The first filtered system was begun in 1865.

5

Even this was not the first water supply system in the city but was built as a response to the unsatisfactory nature of the then existing supply. The previous system simply provided unfiltered water in open masonry ducts. The water from the new plant was treated by sedimentation and filtration.

The opening of the filtered water system in 1870 did not satisfy the needs for water and the older unfiltered system was kept in operation and extended in 1874 and is still in use. It has always been intended that the unfiltered water would be used only for street watering, fire protection, and similar purposes. The complete abandonment of the system has been proposed on a number of occasions. The latest proposal was in the World Health Organization's 1960 report on water supply, sewerage and drainage in the Calcutta Metropolitan District.[2] Each time arguments have prevailed in favour of keeping the unfiltered system in use until the filtered supply becomes adequate for all the city's needs. Despite major extensions to the system, in 1888, 1908, 1923-26, and in 1950, the provision of filtered water has not kept pace with the growth of population even in the corporate city. In addition, there are as many or more people living outside the city boundaries, most without access to a piped water supply.

The total daily public water supply, in the area defined as the Calcutta Metropolitan District, averaged 118 million gallons in 1960, of which 90 million gallons[3] was supplied to the city of Calcutta alone. The remainder of the metropolitan district, with over half the total population of approximately six million, is poorly served by public water supply. There are a number of very small systems, many operated by private manufacturing industry. Even in the city of Calcutta, the supply is insufficient to meet present demands and water is only available intermittently throughout the day. Pressure is low and, even when the water is "on" it is insufficient in most of the system to raise water more than 3 or 4 feet above the ground level. The distribution systems, with a few exceptions, are decayed and cracks in pipes probably lead to contamination of the supply.

---

[2]Abel B. Wolman, et al., "Assignment Report on Water Supply and Sewage Disposal, Greater Calcutta," WHO Project India—170, World Health Organization, Regional Office for Southeast Asia, New Delhi, p. 44. (Mimeographed.)

[3]Measurements of water consumption are in Imperial Gallons.

The existing supply situation results in a number of adjustments by consumers to obtain a more convenient supply of water. The type of adjustment tends to vary according to the level of income and housing:

(a) Pumps and roof tanks. In areas where there is a public supply, most high income households possess pumps to raise the water to rooftop storage tanks. This is done to overcome the problem of low pressure and discontinuity in supply. The pump can also be used to draw water from the distribution system when the pressure would otherwise not permit withdrawals. Where there is no public supply or where an extra water source is necessary to supplement the public supply, households in this income group provide their own source of supply through tube-wells operated by electric pumps.

(b) Water purchase and storage. Middle income households, in areas served by public supply, store water in the house; they do not normally possess roof storage tanks. Elsewhere or to supplement the public supply these households buy water from water sellers or carriers. The carriers obtain their water from public hand operated shallow tubewells.

(c) Reliance on street supplies. The low income sector of the population suffer particularly from the intermittent and unreliable supply presently available. In general, the poor cannot afford to buy water from water carriers but must rely on the water available from street taps or standpipes and the hand operated street tubewells. This water is supplemented from other sources—tanks,[4] shallow wells, the unfiltered water supply system and other locally available surface water sources, including the River Hooghly. Water from these latter sources is generally considered to be "unsafe" and a danger to health.[5]

The existence of the present supply conditions and the adjustments that have resulted probably play a role in the prevalence of high rates of gastro-enteric disease. Mortality from

[4]A tank is an artificial pond normally formed by excavation for building purposes. There are a large number of tanks in Calcutta and they are a very marked feature of the landscape.

[5]Cholera vibrios have been isolated from water samples taken from tanks, the canals, and the River Hooghly; see, A. H. Abou-Gareeb, "The Detection of Cholera Vibrios in Calcutta Waters: The Tanks and Dhobas," Internationales Journal für Prophylaktische Medezin und Sozialhygiene, VI, No. 3 (June, 1962), 65; and S. K. Chatterjee, "The Epidemiological Aspects of Cholera in Calcutta," Indian Journal of Medical Research, LII, No. 8 (August, 1964), 767.

cholera in the Calcutta Metropolitan District is the highest in
West Bengal, well above the average for the state (Table 1).
It has been accepted, moreover, that "Bengal acts as the fons
et origo [source and origin] of cholera."[6] The incidence of
other waterborne diseases is also very high; in the case of dysenteries and general diarrhoeal diseases, it is much higher
(Table 1).

TABLE 1 INCIDENCE OF MORTALITY FROM
CHOLERA AND DYSENTERY, WEST
BENGAL, 1956-60

(Expressed as a Percentage of Total
Deaths)

District	1956	1957	1958	1959	1960
West Bengal					
Cholera	1.78	1.43	1.96	0.68	0.76
Dysentery	3.24	2.76	2.33	3.60	4.36
Howrah*					
Cholera	3.34	2.90	5.28	1.83	1.97
Dysentery	4.22	3.73	3.60	4.29	5.35
Hooghly*					
Cholera	1.47	1.40	2.47	0.48	0.34
Dysentery	3.15	2.57	2.60	3.02	3.64
24-Parganas*					
Cholera	2.96	3.75	4.28	1.46	1.77
Dysentery	4.45	4.57	3.63	4.83	6.20
Calcutta*					
Cholera	2.55	1.55	5.12	1.58	1.65
Dysentery	5.10	4.20	4.91	4.68	4.29
Nadia*					
Cholera	2.13	0.88	0.57	0.03	0.34
Dysentery	2.69	3.38	2.50	3.90	6.64

*Districts within which the Calcutta Metropolitan District is situated.
SOURCE: West Bengal, State Statistical Bureau, Statistical Abstract, 1961 (Alipore:
West Bengal Government Press, 1965).

Water Supply and Public Health

The situation found in Calcutta is repeated in many other
places. The extent of the problem has led to the formulation of
large-scale programmes, both internationally and in the devel-

[6]A. M. Kamal, "Endemicity and Epidemicity of Cholera," Bulletin of the World
Health Organization. XXVIII. No. 3 (1963), 279.

opment plans of individual countries, for the remedying of these deficiencies.[7] The observation of the dichotomy in standards of public health in the developed and underdeveloped countries, and the apparent connection between the raising of the standards of public health and economic growth in the west, has led to claims that water supply systems have an important part to play in the growth process. The role of the water supply system is not seen as being restricted to the humanitarian benefits of better health, including the release of resources devoted to medical services, but beyond that to having economic value in raising the productivity of the labour force and, separately, playing a part in the general process of industrialization.

A high rate of waterborne diseases is characteristic of the tropical underdeveloped countries. In 9 out of 18 of the countries of the Americas, diarrhoeal diseases are the major cause of death and in another three the second cause.[8] It is accepted that the use of impure water plays a part in the transmission of cholera, bacillary dysentery, typhoid and paratyphoid. It is important in the transmission of Salmonella and Shigella infections and amoebiasis. Related features of insufficient public water supply and drainage systems are significant in the occurrence of malaria, filariasis and bilharziasis.

The waterborne diseases are of only minor importance in the more developed nations. In the underdeveloped nations they are the major causes of death (Table 2). The relationship between these diseases and the use of impure water supplies has been well documented. There are many examples from North America and Western Europe in the late nineteenth and early twentieth centuries and more recently from other areas of the world, of the decline in the death rates from these diseases accompanying the introduction of safe and reliable public water supplies. One outstanding example is the gradual reduction of typhoid fever in Massachusetts between 1885 and 1930. During this period the proportion of the population served by a public water supply system rose from 70 per cent to 96 per cent. The death rate from typhoid fell from 40 per 100,000 in 1885 to 1

---

[7]See World Health Organization, "Proceedings and Papers of Inter-Regional Seminar on Integration of Community Water Supplies into Planning of Economic Development," Geneva, September 19-28, 1967. (Mimeographed; to be published.)

[8]Edmund G. Wagner and J. N. Lanoix, Water Supply for Rural Areas and Small Communities, World Health Organization Monograph Series No. 42, p. 16.

9

TABLE 2   DEATHS FROM COMMON WATERBORNE
DISEASES IN SELECTED COUNTRIES

Country	Year	Percentage of Total Deaths				Average Annual Death Rate[a]
		Typhoid	Cholera	Dysentery	Gastritis	
Nigeria						
(Lagos)	1960	–	–	1.7	8.5	1,179.7
UAR[b]	1961	0.3	–	0.1	36.2	1,889.5
Ceylon	1960	0.2	–	0.7	5.0	858.1
Ecuador	1958	1.4	–	0.6	9.0	1,505.1
Mexico	1960	0.7	–	1.2	14.9	1,105.1
Turkey[c]	1962	0.3	–	0.1	9.6	–
Canada	1962	–	–	–	0.6	772.6
U.S.A.	1962	–	–	–	0.5	941.2
Austria	1962	–	–	–	0.7	1,274.6
France	1962	–	–	–	0.8	1,144.1

[a]Number of deaths per 100,000 population.

[b]Statistics are for areas served by Health Bureau, covering approximately
44 per cent of the population.

[c]Statistics only for provincial capitals and district centres.

The statistics for Nigeria, UAR, Ceylon, and Ecuador should be treated
with caution.

SOURCE: United Nations, Statistical Office, Demographic Year Book, 1963 (New York:
UN, 1964), pp. 592–611.

per 100,000 in 1930. It has remained at this level since.[9]

More recently in Japan, the introduction of rural public
water supply systems was accompanied by a fall in the death
rate from intestinal communicable diseases of 28.5 per cent
and in the overall death rate among infants and young children
of 48.3 per cent.[10] A similar reduction in disease was also
noted with the provision and expansion of urban water supply
in the state of Uttar Pradesh, India. In 14 towns, new public
water supply systems were built in the fifteen years from 1940
to 1955. In this period the average reduction in the death rate
from cholera was 74.1 per cent, from typhoid 63.6 per cent,
from dysenteries 23.1 per cent, and from diarrhoeas 42.7 per
cent in the first five years after the construction of the water
supply system.[11]

[9]Modern Sanitation, III, No. 10 (1951), 34.

[10]Japan, Health Statistics (1962), 20.

[11]M. Zaheer, et al., "A Note on Urban Water Supply in Uttar Pradesh," Journal
of the Indian Medical Association, XXXVIII, No. 4 (February, 1962), 181.

The appearance of a link between certain diseases and the absence of a safe, reliable, and sufficient water supply for domestic use has led to a growing concern to remedy the existing situation in the underdeveloped countries. An expansion of water supply facilities is considered necessary. There is a strong feeling in the water supply profession that the needs for water supply are being neglected in the existing aid programmes and national plans of many countries. The profession tends to stress the very large contribution that improvement in water supplies can make to the development process.

> If a single program were chosen which would have the maximum health benefit, which would rapidly stimulate social and economic development, and which would materially improve the standard of living of the people, that program would be water supply with provision for water running into or adjacent to the house.[12]

Present Deficiencies in Public Water Supply Systems

The awareness of the water supply problem and the extent of the deficiencies is not a relatively recent phenomenon. The world wide recognition of the need to remedy the deficiencies is closely connected, however, with the rapid urbanization and stress on development of the last three decades. In India, for example, the population of the five largest metropolitan areas increased by 52 per cent from 1941 to 1951 and by 33 per cent from 1951 to 1961. It is anticipated that the urban population will increase very dramatically by the end of the century.[13] The expansion of the water supply systems has not corresponded to the population increase. The typical existing system neither provides sufficient water nor serves the whole of the urban area. Only a minority of the population have an individ-

[12]Abraham Horowitz, Director, Pan-American Health Organization, quoted by Abel Wolman and H. M. Bosch, "U.S. Water Supply Lessons Applicable to Developing Countries," Journal of the American Water Works Association, LV, No. 8 (August, 1963), 954.

[13]See K. Davis, "Urbanization in India: Past and Future," in India's Urban Future, ed. by R. Turner, pp. 3-26.

TABLE 3 URBAN WATER SUPPLY, 1962, SERVED AND
UNSERVED POPULATION, BY REGION*

(Population in Thousands)

| Region | Urban Population Supplied | | | | | | Urban Population Not Served | |
| | From House Connections | | From Public Outlets | | Total Served | | | |
	No.	%	No.	%	No.	%	No.	%
North Africa	10650	57	3700	20	14350	77	4190	23
Africa south of Sahara	2780	13	8060	38	10840	51	10150	49
Africa, Sub-Total	13430	34	11760	30	25190	64	14340	36
Central America and Caribbean	15690	55	8550	30	24240	85	4270	15
Tropical South America	30830	59	14000	27	44830	86	7150	14
Temperate South America	14880	67	4930	22	19810	89	2440	11
Latin America, Sub-Total	61400	60	27480	27	88880	87	13860	13
Southwest Asia	10220	39	9475	36	19695	75	6575	25
South Central Asia	13320	14	19350	20	32670	34	62570	66
Southeast Asia	5965	15	10635	26	16600	41	24190	59
East Asia	3010	20	4720	30	7730	50	7720	50
Asia, Sub-Total	32515	18	44180	25	76695	43	101055	57
TOTAL	107345	33	83420	26	190765	59	129255	41

*SOURCE: Bernd H. Dieterich and John M. Henderson, Urban Water
Supply Conditions and Needs in Seventy-Five Developing Countries, World Health
Organization Public Health Paper No. 23 (Geneva: WHO, 1963).

ual house connection.[14] A large number may share a tap with
other families in the same building. A substantial minority of
the urban population are unserved or are dependent on public
water sources. The overall global situation has probably
changed little from that reported by the World Health Organization in 1962 (Table 3).

Latin America is the only developing region where over
half the urban population is served by house connections. In
South Central Asia, the World Health Organization region which

---

[14] There are only 100,000 connections to the Calcutta Corporation water supply system in a city of 3 million people.

includes India, over two-thirds of the urban population have no access to a public supply system. In many cases, even where the population is served by house connections, the water provided may be either deficient in quality or intermittent in supply.

The Prevailing Strategy of
Improvement Programmes

Recognition of the scale of the urban water supply problem has led to a significant amount of interest by a number of international bodies. The World Health Organization, the International Bank for Reconstruction and Development, the Agency for International Development of the US State Department and similar agencies in other countries have all become involved in the solution of the problem. The basis of this concern is the serious health hazard which can be traced to the present deficiencies in urban water supplies. The World Health Organization and the Agency for International Development have both suggested a world wide programme for the provision of water supply. Such programmes would require considerable external financial support. The total cost of water supply provision to close the gap between the existing level of supply and needs in urban areas has been estimated at 4.2 billion dollars over the period 1961-1975. How much of this amount would be provided by foreign aid is not known.[15]

World Health Organization (WHO). —Concern over present standards of the World Health Organization led to the proposal at the Twelfth World Health Assembly in 1959 for a special "spearhead" environmental health programme.[16] The core of this programme became the provision of piped water supplies under the "Community Water Supply Programme." Goals and standards have been proposed on the basis of the findings of a survey of existing conditions in seventy-five developing countries. The purpose of the survey was to estimate the current

---

[15] An estimate of the costs of a global water supply programme was made for the Agency for International Development by Henderson in 1961 (John M. Henderson, "Report on the Global Urban Water Supply Program, Costs in Developing Nations, 1961-1975," International Cooperation Administration, Washington, D.C., June, 1961, 99 pp.). (Mimeographed.)

[16] Bernd H. Dieterich and John M. Henderson, Urban Water Supply Conditions and Needs in Seventy-Five Developing Countries, World Health Organization Public Health Paper No. 23, p. 9.

status of urban water supplies and the estimated future needs.

The original proposal, as outlined at the Twelfth World Health Assembly, was concerned with community water supply. A community was defined as "an aggregation of houses which by virtue of their proximity may be economically served by a piped water supply system."[17] The minimum population of a community was set at 1,000 people. In countries where rural populations are agglomerated, this meant that the programme would cover both rural and urban areas. The specific proposals made by the World Health Organization, however, are concerned solely with the building of piped water supply systems in urban areas. The distinction was made on the assumption that the provision of water in urban areas would be more relevant to economic development and improvements in public health, and that developing countries could take care of their own rural water supply.

Great variations in the needs of individual countries, and in their capacity to fulfil these needs, prevented the formulation of a specific programme of water supply development on a global scale. Instead, the World Health Organization proposed a number of goals to guide individual country programmes to improve and expand existing water supply facilities.

The programme is divided into two parts —a set of intermediate goals to be achieved by 1977 and a set of ultimate goals to be reached at an unspecified later date. The high standards set for the ultimate goals preclude any possibility of generalizing rates of achievement between countries. The ultimate goals are:

1. Piped water supply should be provided to all premises.
2. Adequate service should be maintained at all times.
3. Water for drinking, household, and other purposes should be provided in adequate volume.
4. Standards for drinking water quality should be adopted and enforced that would be no less rigid than those set by the World Health Organization.[18]
5. Water sources should be protected against pollution.

---

[17]World Health Organization, Regional Office for Southeast Asia, "Community Water Supplies: The Position of Southeast Asia Region," Working Paper No. 1, Fifteenth Session, Regional Committee, New Delhi, 1962. (Mimeographed.)

[18]These standards are given in World Health Organization, International Standards for Drinking Water, p. 21.

6. Water schemes should be administered independently and according to sound management practices.

7. Regular revenues should be established to cover operation, maintenance, capital charges, and depreciation.[19]

It was realized that the magnitude of the problem was such that these objectives were not realistic if any progress was to be made in the near future. Therefore, an interim set of objectives were defined to be reached by 1977.

(a) Piped water should be supplied within fifteen years (1962-1977) to all people living in urban communities either through house connections or by public outlets within a reasonable distance from each home.

(b) During this period of fifteen years the percentage of people served from house connections should be increased at a rate appropriate to local conditions.

(c) An adequate volume of water should be provided through a non-intermittent service maintaining a suitable minimum pressure at all times (p. 24).

These goals allow a considerable flexibility in the application of the programme to a specific country. They are so general as not to provide guides to the appropriate levels of supply or of the size of any proposed programmes. The establishment of the goals does, at least, invite investigation of what "adequate" service and volumes of supply might be under varying circumstances.

The World Health Organization programmes also suggest a solution to the financial and managerial problems which are an important aspect of the whole water supply question. The major suggestion is that water supply should be recognized as a national, as well as a local, concern (p. 63). Water supply schemes should be adopted into national planning programmes. A national water supply policy should be formulated. The policy should identify and stress the urgency of water supply problems, and should make their solution a major aim of all government programmes, for the promotion of development (p. 64). The suggested agency for this amalgamation would be the local independent water board. The form and role of this organization is not spelled out in the original report but an ex-

---

[19]Dieterich and Henderson, Urban Water Supply, p. 63.

ample is the newly established Calcutta Metropolitan Water Supply, Sewerage and Drainage Authority, intermediate between the State Government and the local authorities.[20]

The World Health Organization is primarily an international technical body and it does not provide financial aid. It functions only in an advisory capacity and plays no direct part in the construction and operation of water supply systems. The normal method of operation is to provide the services of consulting engineers to prepare feasibility studies, master plans, and some detailed design work. The consulting engineer will work in cooperation with a local agency. The cost of the consulting engineers is met through the United Nations Development Programme or the Special Fund.

WHO attempts to meet the engineering and financial feasibility criteria of the aid or lending agency. Thus the financial feasibility of projects is not really the responsibility of WHO but rather that of the actual institution providing financial aid.[21]

The interest of WHO mainly arises from a concern with the standard of public health. The impression is that other considerations would play a lesser part but for the insistence of aid or lending agencies on the necessity for schemes to be financially viable.

The Agency for International Development (AID). —The one other major aid agency concerned with water supply problems on a global scale is the Agency for International Development, formerly the International Cooperation Administration, of the US State Department. The interests of AID are wider than those of the World Health Organization in the sense that they extend to the actual construction and management of water supply systems, but narrower in the sense that they are more directly subject to the foreign policy interests of the United States. AID, for various reasons, has concentrated its efforts heavily on Latin America.

The policies of AID for water supply development are very similar to those of the WHO. There is perhaps some difference in the amount of emphasis the Agency places on the operation of

---

[20]Wolman, "Assignment Report," p. 36.

[21]Interview with Bernd H. Dieterich, Sanitary Engineer, Department of Environmental Health, World Health Organization, Geneva, July, 1966

water supply systems as public utilities on a commercial basis.[22] The basic points of the programme are:

(a) Water supply systems should be considered as a public utility in the same way as electricity, gas, or telephone systems. The users or beneficiaries should pay the full cost of supplying water.

(b) Community water supply development and management should be the responsibility of a single agency, preferably at the municipal or metropolitan level. In less developed countries this may not be feasible and the responsibility for water supply should lie in the hands of an autonomous national or regional agency.

(c) The national or state public health agency should have a basic responsibility for the provision of public water supply. It should be the primary agent of government for the promotion of community water supplies since the lack of water, in most underdeveloped countries, constitutes a major health hazard. The control of public water supplies should not lie with general water resource agencies.[23]

AID has shown considerable interest in the quantitative relationship between economic development and the demand for domestic water supply. This interest has extended both to the economic benefits to be expected from the building of water supply systems and levels of per capita demand at different levels of income. As in the World Health Organization's programme, however, no specific conclusions have yet been reached on the nature of these relationships.

In essence, both the World Health Organization's programme and that of AID are only a frame of reference within which specific programmes may be developed. One of these programmes, India's National Water Supply and Sanitation Programme, is examined in more detail.

India's National Water Supply and Sanitation Programme. — The Indian programme is significant for three reasons. It has

---

[22]Utility operation of water supplies is the only one of these guidelines that has been consistently followed (personal communication from A. H. Holloway, Chief, Community Water Supply Branch, Office of War on Hunger, Agency for International Development, U.S. State Department, November, 1967).

[23]United States, State Department, International Cooperation Administration, "Report of the Panel of Expert Consultants to the International Cooperation Administration on the Community Water Supply Development Program," Washington, D.C., April, 12-14, 1960, pp. 20-21. (Mimeographed.)

been operating, although with mixed success, for a relatively long time. Secondly, India is "the individual country with the greatest requirements . . . where it is estimated at the present time 56.7 million urban dwellers need new or extended water supplies and 15 million need on-premises service."[24] Finally, it is regarded as a model example of a national programme.

The National Water Supply and Sanitation Programme was begun in 1954, in the last year of the First Five Year Plan. The programme was developed, with the encouragement of WHO, due to the inability of the municipalities and states to cope with water supply requirements and the haphazard and spasmodic nature in which the existing schemes had been implemented.[25]

The intention of the Indian National Programme is to assist the prosecution of existing schemes and not to replace them. It is concerned with both urban and rural water supply and sanitation. There was also need to enforce some standard of technical competence through central supervision. Certain goals were laid down for urban water supply in the Second and Third Five Year Plans, in terms of priorities. The suggested priorities were, in the following order: (1) municipal areas which do not have protected water supply arrangements, (2) improvements and expansion of inadequate or unsafe supply systems, (3) Pilgrim centres, and (4) areas with piped water supply but which require a new or improved sewerage system.[26] The extent of the programme has been set by the allocation of specific amounts of money during the different Five Year Plan periods. The amounts have increased in each plan (Table 4).

The determination of the nature and the size of water supply development was still left, however, largely in the hands of the states and ultimately, of the municipalities. The latter are responsible for the original proposals for water supply schemes. Paradoxically, actual expenditure, for reasons that will be discussed later, fell short of the monies allocated.

---

[24]Wolman, "Assignment Report," p. 48.

[25]India, Committee on Plan Projects, Report on National Water Supply and Sanitation Schemes, p. 1.

[26]India, Planning Commission, Third Five Year Plan (1961), p. 655.

TABLE 4   FINANCIAL ALLOCATIONS TO URBAN WATER SUPPLY
UNDER THE NATIONAL WATER SUPPLY AND SANITA-
TION PROGRAMME IN DIFFERENT FIVE-YEAR PLANS

Plan	Years	U.S. Dollars (millions)	Amount (crores Rs.)[a]
First	1951–56	1.7	12.75
Second	1956–61	8.5	63.00
Third	1961–66	11.5	86.00

[a] 1 crore = 10,000,000 rupees (Rs.).

SOURCE: India, Committee on Plan Projects, Report on National Water Supply
and Sanitation Schemes (New Delhi: Government of India Press, 1961).

The Role of Water Supply
in Economic Development

The provision of water supply systems is part of the process of economic and social development. If there is a link between the establishment of a public water supply system and a
quickening of economic progress, in what way and at what scale
should the water supply systems be built? How can the development of water supply systems be directed to aid the growth
process in an optimal fashion? The existing programmes for
water supply development discussed in the previous section are
based on the assumption that water supply systems have a critical role to play in development beyond that of the impact on the
level of public health. Dieterich and Henderson, in their paper
outlining the extent of the needs for water supply in the developing countries, emphasize the developmental role of public
water supply systems.

Water supply has become a critical factor in public
health and economic development in most parts of
the world, particularly in the developing countries.
Deficiencies and backlogs have created conditions
that call for immediate efforts by governments and
local agencies to promote the construction of new
supplies. Also, the influence of water supplies on
conditions of health and economic progress through-

19

out the world opens up a wide field for action by
international bodies concerned with such problems.[27]

Emphasis is placed on the provision of water as a public
health measure but there has also been a considerable concern
in recent years with the wider role of piped water as an economic commodity.[28] Water supply systems are conceived of as
having more than a direct public health role to play in the process of economic development.

The precise nature of the contributions that water supply
might make beyond public health is not clear. In a Seminar on
the Financing and Management of Water and Sewerage Works
held in New Delhi, water supply systems were referred to as
"the springboard for progress in every activity which improves
the material and mental well-being of man."[29] In such a statement as this there is perhaps an exaggeration of the position of
water supplies, but it does embody a seemingly widespread view
of the impact water supplies may have on economic development.
The urging of the need for the provision of water supplies is
made in the absence of any definition of their specific role.
There is a tendency to assume that they are important in general terms because of the relationship between safe water and
less disease. Even where there is a detailed discussion of the
problems of providing water supply, there is no definite notion
of the required levels of supply, types of organization, or condi-
tion of supply which should apply in varying situations.

Planning the provision of water supply has been, and is,
very much on an ad hoc basis. A few general tenets do appear
to be held, however, mostly derived from western experience.

Western Experience of
Water Supply Systems

The development of public water supply systems in the
western countries has largely been undertaken by municipal

---

[27]Dieterich and Henderson, Urban Water Supply, p. 9.

[28] For example see the speech by Wolman to the opening session of meeting of the
Panel of Expert Consultants held by the International Cooperation Administration in
Washington, D.C., April, 12-14, 1960.

[29]India, Ministry of Health, Proceedings and Recommendations, Seminar on Financing and Management of Water and Sewerage Works, p. 15.

governments with a limited amount of private participation. The private water companies, by necessity, and the municipal undertakings, by choice, have both operated on commercial lines in the sense that they are self-financing. Most water supply organizations raise and clear their own debt in addition to covering operating and maintenance costs from their revenues. The way the supply was provided and the welfare considerations that largely underlay the decisions to construct piped distribution systems led to what can be called the "abundance criterion." This approach to the provision of water supply grew out of the cheapness of water and the efficacy of safe piped supplies in combating disease. The emphasis was on encouraging the use of water. In many respects this emphasis still remains today. It was usual to build the water system large enough to ensure against shortage and to provide in advance for predicted population increases. Once the system was built, water use was encouraged by low charges, even in systems where the water was sold through meters, in order to raise revenue to clear the capital debt.[30]

Water supply systems may be run on commercial lines in the sense that they are financially self-supporting but there has been little interest shown in the economics of water supply. This lack of interest can be traced to three factors: (1) the ease with which urban water supply systems were built and financed,[31] (2) the low economic cost of urban water supply compared to its value in use; the marginal value of water is low despite its large aggregate value in use, and (3) the lack of any major public-private conflict over water used for urban water supply.[32]

The important differences here between the developed and underdeveloped countries lie in the first factor. The other factors are common to the water supply situation in both cases. The marginal value of water is only likely to be high in conditions of extreme scarcity. Public-private conflict over the wa-

---

[30]See for example the discussion in J. J. Warford, "Water 'Requirements': The Investment Decision in the Water Supply Industry," The Manchester School of Economic and Social Studies, XXXIV, No. 1 (January, 1966), 87-106.

[31]Wolman and Bosch, "U.S. Water Supply Lessons Applicable to Developing Countries," 948.

[32]Jerome W. Milliman, "Policy Horizons for Future Urban Water Supply," Land Economics, XLIX, No. 2 (May, 1963), 110.

ter used for urban supply is growing but it is more of a feature of the developed industrialized west than the underdeveloped countries. In contrast with western countries in the nineteenth century, urban water supply systems cannot be easily built, for both technical or financial reasons, in most developing countries today. There are severe restraints on the amounts of capital and administrative and managerial ability available. There are few or no reputable and experienced consulting firms and often the construction firms are untested in following large and complex designs. This together with a number of other characteristics of the urban environment places considerable difficulties in the path of transferring western experience and techniques of water supply provision without modification.

Water Supply and Social Overhead Capital Investment

It is not the role of public water supply systems in the process of economic development itself that is open to question. Economic growth and the accompanying urbanization require the provision of safe water supplies to maintain tolerable public health standards. Very high incidences of disease would produce destructive stresses in any society. It is the magnitude and timing of investment and the nature of the supply systems which are open to question. It is also unclear as to whether there are benefits other than improvements in health. Even the latter above an unspecified minimum can be disputed on economic grounds.

A water supply system is part of that category of economic activities subsumed under the heading of the social infrastructure or social overhead capital. These are activities which in themselves are not directly productive but are the necessary basis for the successful growth of productive activities. The term social overhead capital is normally applied to such disparate activities as education, electricity, the transportation system, health services, systems of administration as well as various aspects of water development among which urban water supplies are only a part. ·Attitudes towards the place of social overhead capital in the economic growth process vary considerably. The need for social overhead facilities is one which

22

cannot be disputed but debates on their importance leave room for considerable doubt and uncertainty.

A number of questions have been raised about the level of investment that should be made in social overhead or infrastructure facilities. The breakdown of gross fixed investment in an advanced economy (as estimated by Lewis) is shown in Table 5.

TABLE 5 GROSS FIXED INVESTMENT
IN AN ADVANCED ECONOMY

Sector	Percentage of Total
Housing	25
Public Works and Utilities	30
Manufacturing and Agriculture	30
Other Commercial	10

SOURCE: W. Arthur Lewis, Theory of Economic Growth (London: Unwin, 1955), p. 210.

Social overhead investment, including housing, commonly accounts for over half the total of all investment. This is so in an advanced economy with a large existing stock of social overhead capital. In an underdeveloped economy, this stock does not exist and one might expect a policy of heavy initial investment in the social infrastructure.

> There is reason to believe that the proportion [of social overhead investment] is particularly high in the first decades of development and declines thereafter. This is because initial development calls for the establishment of a framework of utilities, and though it is necessary to spend money on maintaining and improving and extending the framework, it is possible that these later expenditures are relatively not so heavy as those which have initially to be made. [33]

An investigation of United Nations information on the composition of investment in different countries does not bear out

---

[33] W. Arthur Lewis, Theory of Economic Growth, p. 211.

TABLE 6 COMPARATIVE LEVELS OF SOCIAL OVERHEAD INVESTMENT

Country	Gross Domestic Product Per Capita 1962 (U.S. $)	Mining and Manufacturing as Per Cent GDP 1960	Percentage Share of Overheads in GDCF, [g] 1960
Tanganyika	60	11.0	37.9
Thailand	93[a]	12.0	31.2
Sudan	94	4.9	37.0
Korea	105[b]	12.2	42.3
Rhodesia and Nyasaland	147	33.8	38.6
Philippines	191[b]	17.4	52.1
Portugal	279	38.7[c]	34.0
Greece	394	20.1	52.0
Jamaica	419	21.9	13.7[d]
Ireland	641	30.4[e]	36.3
Italy	688	33.5	31.9
Venezuela	901	42.2	37.3
Belgium	1215	33.4	31.5
United Kingdom	1288	39.9	34.2
Norway	1316	27.5	49.5
Australia	1416	30.4	37.7
Canada	1807	30.5	45.7
United States	2691	30.9	33.5[f]

Overhead investment includes Public Utilities (electricity, gas, and water), Transportation and Communications, Public Administration and Service Industries.

[a] 1961

[b] 1958

[c] Including construction and utilities.

[d] Not including transportation.

[e] Including construction.

[f] Not including service industries.

[g] Gross Domestic Capital Formation.

SOURCE: United Nations, Yearbook of National Account Statistics, 1963 (New York: UN, 1964).

this assertion (Table 6). It would seem that in practice, as other economists have suggested, there is a tendency to minimize the investment in the social infrastructure in many countries.[34] If this is to be the basis of policy towards social investment there need to be tests to establish the optimum level

---

[34] See for example the comments of Albert O. Hirschmann, The Strategy of Economic Development, pp. 83-97; and Jan Tinbergen, The Design of Development, pp. 29-45.

of investment. In general terms these tests would probably be something akin to Tinbergen's complementary test within a framework of assigned goals for national welfare.[35]

Such investment is characterized by a lengthy gestation lag between the original investment and the beginning of a return. The very nature of the activities undertaken accounts for this lag. It is most marked in education but holds for all types of social overhead investment. The contribution of these activities is, in addition, very dependent upon the development of the related productive activities. Investment in social overhead facilities is largely made in the public sector due to these long gestation periods and the size of the individual projects. In India, public investment in this sector accounted for 88 per cent of the total in the period 1951 to 1960.[36] Investment in water supply is normally entirely within the public sector in all countries.

A comparative study of the levels of, and apparent needs for, social overhead investment provides little knowledge about the role of social overhead investment in the growth process. Detailed knowledge of the impact of specific facilities can only be gained from the study of the particular problems facing individual countries.

In the west the development of urban water supplies showed what can be described as a permissive sequence—permissive in the sense that the expansions to the systems were made with little attempt to evaluate the benefits to be gained from an increased consumption of water. Water for domestic supply was, and still is to a very large extent, not treated as an economic commodity. Such an approach is in every case of doubtful validity or wisdom but it is particularly so in the underdeveloped countries with their shortages of capital and high rates of return on investments.

There is a strong priority basis, therefore, for the argument that the expansion of water supply facilities will be closer to an optimum rate if the amount of water supplied is kept at a level sufficient for the prevention of waterborne diseases. It

---

[35]Tinbergen, The Design of Development, pp. 31-32.

[36]J. M. Healey, The Development of Social Overhead Capital in India, 1950-1960, p. 11. Healey only includes power, transportation, and communications in his definition of social overhead capital; with the wider definition taken here the proportion of public investment would be higher.

is not a practical proposition to plan for a system with individual house connections, at western levels of supply, just because the present water supply system is inadequate. Such a system should only be provided if it can be established that the return, in regard to both economic and social benefits, is greater than it would be with the construction of smaller systems.

There is a need to be able to compare the anticipated returns from the development of water supply systems of different sizes. A comparison of this type is possible, even if difficult, through the use of benefit-cost analysis. The analysis has already been applied to water supply facilities in the development situation and these will be discussed below.

Attempts to Quantify the Benefits of Public Water Supplies

The use of benefit-cost analysis in determining decisions on water supply and similar programmes aids not only in the testing of the financial return and feasibility of any project but also in the determination of the nature and the size of the benefits that can be expected.[37] The analysis may show that the major benefits are of a type which it is difficult to express in financial terms. Financially it may not be possible to justify the project but the results of the project may still meet other criteria and be justifiable on the grounds of social policy. Once the benefits have been realized in this way, it would be possible to direct all efforts to producing the benefits as fully and rapidly as possible.

A number of studies have been made in a rather general way to determine the actual economic benefits that an increased or new public water supply will provide. These studies have largely been limited to the apparent decrease in the occurrence of disease which can be identified with the introduction of safe

---

[37]Probably the best concise outline of the principles and techniques of benefit-cost analysis, although rather a simplified one is, W. R. D. Sewell, J. Davis, A. D. Scott, and D. W. Ross, Guide to Benefit-Cost Analysis, prepared for the Resources for Tomorrow Conference held in Montreal, October 23-28, 1961 (Ottawa: Queen's Printer, 1962), 49 pp. See also, United Nations, Research Institute for Social Development, "Cost-Benefit Analysis of Social Projects," Report No. 7, Geneva, April, 1966, 129 pp. (Mimeographed.) Both these sources contain valuable bibliographies.

and reliable supplies of water. These studies suggest that the greatest benefits are in the prevention of premature deaths from waterborne diseases.[38] A study, in Venezuela, of the anticipated benefits from the provision of public water supplies in rural areas, assumed the annual benefits to be as follows:

1. 75 per cent of the value of earnings lost due to premature deaths, Bolivars, 94,521,766 (US $21,004,830).
2. 75 per cent of the value of earnings lost due to illness, Bolivars, 1,740,384 (US $386,752).
3. 75 per cent of the cost of medicine and medical supplies,[39] Bolivars, 1,232,009 (US $273,779).
4. 100 per cent of the cost of water bought from vendors or carried from streams, Bolivars, 73,000,000 (US $16,222,222).

The total annual benefits amount to some 170 million bolivars (US $38 million), while the total annual cost of providing the system was estimated at 22 million bolivars (US $5 million).[40] This results in a very favourable benefit-cost ratio. There are, however, a number of questions that can be raised about the form of the analysis and this will be taken up below. At this point it is sufficient to take note of the very large mortality benefits. A similar result is found in the study by Atkins of rural water supply, although his calculations are less precise.[41]

The benefit-cost analysis by Pyatt and Rogers of the investment in public water supplies in Puerto Rico is a more rigorous analysis than the previous studies discussed. Here, also,

---

[38]Edmund G. Wagner and Luis Wannoni, "Anticipated Savings in Venezuela through the Construction of Safe Water Supplies in Rural Areas" (paper presented to the Expert Committee on Environmental Sanitation, World Health Organization, Geneva, July 27-31, 1953); Charles H. Atkins, "Some Economic Aspects of Sanitation Programs in Rural Areas and Small Towns" (paper presented to the Expert Committee on Environmental Sanitation, World Health Organization, Geneva, July 27-31, 1953); Edwin E. Pyatt and Peter P. Rogers, "On Estimating Benefit-Cost Ratios for Water Supply Investments," American Journal of Public Health, LII, No. 10 (October, 1962), 1729-1742.

[39]Only 75 per cent of the calculated costs of deaths and illness were used, as one-quarter of the population was already served by public water supply systems. Presumably the remaining cost of the disease cannot be claimed against deficient water supplies.

[40]Wagner and Wannoni, paper presented to the World Health Organization, July 27-31, 1953, p. 12.

[41]Atkins, paper presented to the World Health Organization, July 27-31, 1953, p. 6.

mortality benefits were found to be the major component of the expected benefits.[42] Unlike the previous papers the benefit-cost ratio was found to be very low in Puerto Rico. During the first ten years of the operation of the water supply system, it would be less than unity, although if the benefits to industry of a public water supply were added to the public health benefits, then the ratio might reach unity. Industrial benefits were found to be relatively slight particularly in the early years of the life of the system.[43] After the tenth year the ratio exceeds unity, and by the end of its useful life the ratio reaches 2.5.[44]

The studies support the view that water supply yields primarily public health benefits and through the improvements in the level of health, gives considerable benefits in economic terms. The assumptions made in the analysis discussed are open to question. The two studies of rural water supplies give only very crude approximations of the quantitative values that can be attached to a human life. In neither study was a discount rate used and therefore no comparison made with other investment opportunities. In the Puerto Rico study the discount rate was taken as 4 per cent. The analysis was also performed with a discount rate of 10 per cent and in this case the benefit-cost ratio did not reach unity at any time.[45]

A 4 per cent discount rate is a low rate for use in an underdeveloped country. The discount rate should not only reflect the interest rate at which the government or any other agency may be able to borrow money, but must also take into account social opportunity costs—the returns realizable by the same investment outside the limits of the particular project under review.[46]

[42] Pyatt and Rogers, "On Estimating Benefit-Cost Ratios for Water Supply Investments," 1740.

[43] Pyatt, Rogers, and Hassan Sheikh, "Benefit-Cost Analysis for Municipal Water Supplies," Land Economics, XL, No. 4 (November, 1964), 445.

[44] Pyatt and Rogers, "On Estimating Benefit-Cost Ratios for Water Supply Investments," 1742.

[45] Pyatt, Rogers, and Sheikh. "Benefit-Cost Analysis for Municipal Water Supplies," 447.

[46] For a discussion of appropriate discount rates, see M. M. Kelso, "Economic Analysis in the Allocation of the Federal Budget to Resource Development," in Water Resource Development, ed. by S. C. Smith and E. N. Castle, pp. 72-73; Jack Hirshliefer, James C. DeHaven and Jerome W. Milliman, Water Supply: Economics, Technology, and Policy, pp. 139-151; see for examples, J. Krutilla and O. Eckstein, Multiple Purpose River Development, especially chap. iv; and Hirshliefer, DeHaven, and Milliman, Water Supply, p. 171.

The social opportunity costs are probably very high in a developing economy. The marginal utility of consumption would be greater at lower absolute levels of consumption and there would, therefore, be a strong preference for present over future consumption unless political concerns dictated otherwise. Such a situation has been shown by Harbeger's study of market interest rates in India. Harbeger concludes that the rate of return of investments in industries in India in 1959 ranged up to over 200 per cent.[47] These are private rates but lead to the suspicion that the social opportunity cost of public investment would be high, if not this high. A benefit-cost analysis would need, therefore, very high discount rates to reflect the true social time preference or opportunity cost rate. Given the need to use high discount rates and the knowledge of the expected benefits from the experience of the Puerto Rican study, it is doubtful that piped water supply projects can be justified in terms of the traditional approach to benefit-cost analysis, measuring the contribution of the project to national income.

The basis of all the attempts that have been made to quantify the benefits from the public water supply systems has been the economic value of a human life. This value can be calculated from the present value of net future earnings of different age groups in the population. A modification of this concept is used in Pyatt's Puerto Rican study. The concept was originally developed in work done in connection with the calculation of benefits from general health programmes.[48] The present value of earnings is measured by the value of total future earnings less total future consumption discounted back to the present time. Pyatt's study used average earnings according to age group. Using average earnings may overestimate the economic worth of the section of the population liable to waterborne diseases. Studies in Calcutta show, as is to be expected, that the lowest income groups have a higher rate of these diseases than the population

---

[47]A. C. Harbeger, "Cost-Benefit Analysis and Economic Growth," The Economic Weekly (Bombay). Annual Number (1962), 207-222.

[48]See L. I. Dublin and A. J. Lotka, The Money Value of a Man; more recently it has been used in Burton A. Wiesbrod, Economics of Public Health, particularly pp. 40-70.

as a whole.[49] Recalculation of the level of benefits allowing for this bias would considerably lower the size of the benefits.

Possibly even more significant, from the viewpoint of the place of water supply systems in development, than the criticisms that have already been made, is the limitation inherent in the type of benefit-cost analyses that have been performed. A benefit-cost analysis confined solely to the provision of a water supply system, where there was not one before, adds little to the understanding of the role of water supply systems in economic development. If the analysis is to be really effective, changes in the demand for water as economic growth proceeds and per capita incomes rise must be understood. The problem in the provision of water supply is not simply that the provision of water is beneficial in itself. If there is to be a rational expansion of water supply facilities, it is necessary to know what the anticipated demands are likely to be as incomes rise and associated improvements in the living environment occur. Similarly, how do patterns of water use and demand vary as society moves from being predominantly rural to more urban, and from smaller to larger cities, apart from changes in housing and income? Further, how is the spatial pattern of water demand within the city likely to change as improvements in the living environment occur?

The prediction of the future pattern of water demand is not possible without information about the complex of uses which make up the demand for water. The future levels of consumption, as the available supply is increased, will depend upon the extent that the use of water is related to the price of water,[50] family income, type of housing, and other social, economic, and cultural influences. In a city in an underdeveloped country, variations in these factors may produce considerable differences in the urban area.

---

[49]In Calcutta there is a positive relationship between the proportion of the bustee (slum) population in a ward and the level of the endemicity rate for cholera, Abou-Gareeb, "Trends of Mortality from Cholera in Calcutta City Wards during Study Period of 21 Years," Calcutta Medical Journal, LVII, No. 2 (June, 1960), 187; see also, Abou-Gareeb, "The Detection of Cholera Endemic Centres in Calcutta City," ibid., No. 3 (October, 1960), 343-353.

[50]The price of water may not only be reflected in an actual cost per unit of water supplied but also in the amount of effort expended in collecting water for domestic use when there is no, or only a skeletal, public water supply system.

The Relationship of Water Consumption to Socio-Economic Factors

Water demand per capita, or the anticipated levels of water consumption, is one of the most important variables used in the design and planning of water supply systems. Variation in the level of water consumption is not just a random process and it can be shown that different classes of consumers place consistently differing demands on the water supply system.

Analysis of the overall variations in average per capita water use between cities in the United States showed that variations in water demand followed a systematic pattern.[51] In areas with metered supplies, the level of per capita consumption could be determined from a number of independent variables. The variables included the price of water, the climate, and interrelated socio-economic factors subsumed under the size of the town or the number of persons per meter.[52]

The importance of socio-economic differences between residential consumers in determining levels of per capita demand is emphasized in more detailed studies on a smaller scale. One such study was undertaken into differences in water demand among the smaller municipalities of the North Eastern Illinois Metropolitan Area (Chicago).[53]

From this study the most important underlying factors influencing water demand appeared to be the proportion of single unit structures, the proportion of two unit structures, and the proportion of industrial water use in a municipality. Variations in the proportion of types of residential housing are a reflection of the social and economic difference between the populations of the different communities.

---

[51] Many of these studies were based on data derived from the American Water Works Association Survey of Water Works in 1955 (American Water Works Association, Staff Report, "A Survey of Operating Data for Water Works in 1955," Journal of the American Water Works Association, XLIX, No. 5 [May, 1955], 553-696).

[52] These studies include, R. Porges, "Factors Influencing Per Capita Water Consumption," Water and Sewage Works, CIV, No. 5 (May, 1957), 199-204; Louis Fourt, "Forecasting the Urban Residential Demand for Water," Agricultural Economics Seminar, University of Chicago, Department of Economics, February, 1958, 9 pp. (Mimeographed.)

[53] Shue Tuck Wong, John R. Sheaffer, and Harold B. Gotass, "A Multivariate Statistical Analysis of Water Supplies" (paper presented at the American Society of Civil Engineers, Water Resources Engineering Conference, Milwaukee, Wisconsin, May 14, 1963), 17 pp. (Mimeographed.)

Investigations of water consumption at the level of the individual household have shown that the consumption varies with the standard of living and the size of the family.[54] Income differences as a factor in variations in per capita demand were less significant than housing conditions. The relationship of the amounts of water consumption is particularly strong in the United States to differences in lot size, illustrating the importance of lawn irrigation in high levels of water consumption.[55] Wolff found that in the older central areas of the city, water use averaged 65 gallons per capita but in the newer suburban areas, with larger houses and lots, use averaged 125 gallons per capita a day.[56]

The most thorough investigation of factors affecting residential water use is that of the members of the Residential Water Use Research Project at Johns Hopkins University. This study has produced the best available set of demand prediction equations.[57] The basic conclusion of this study is that residential demands depend directly on the economic level of the consumers and the potential evapotranspiration for the period of demand in question.[58]

The impact of price on residential demand was further investigated by Howe and Linaweaver using data collected in the Johns Hopkins study.[59] Howe and Linaweaver separated domestic use from lawn sprinkling use.[60] It was found that domestic demand was quite price inelastic but strongly affected by population density, measured by the number of persons per dwelling.[61]

[54]D. F. Dunn and T. E. Larson, "Relationship of Domestic Water Use to Assessed Valuation, with Selected Demographic and Socio-Economic Variables," Journal of the American Water Works Association, LV, No. 4 (April, 1963), 441-449.

[55]J. B. Wolff, "Forecasting Residential Water Requirements," Journal of the American Water Works Association, XLIX, No. 3 (March, 1957), 225-235.

[56]Ibid., 227

[57]F. P. Linaweaver, Jr., J. C. Geyer, and J. B. Wolff, "Final and Summary Report on Phase Two of Residential Water Use Research Project," Department of Environmental Engineering Science, Johns Hopkins University, June, 1966. (Mimeographed.)

[58]Linaweaver, Jr., "Report II, Phase Two, Residential Water Use Research Project," Sanitary Engineering and Water Resources, Johns Hopkins University, Baltimore, June, 1965, pp. 25-50. (Mimeographed.)

[59]Charles W. Howe and Linaweaver, Jr., "The Impact of Price on Residential Water Demand," Water Resources Research, III, No. 1 (1967), 13-32.

[60]Ibid., 16.

[61]Ibid., 27.

Sprinkling use demands showed greater price inelasticity and appreciable income elasticity but the degree of elasticity was affected by aridity. Sprinkling demands were relatively inelastic in the dry Western areas of the United States and elastic in the more humid East.[62]

If it is accepted that water consumption is related to social and economic variables as well as the price, the notion can be more generally applied. It can be anticipated that there would be differences in water consumption between countries at different levels of development, as expressed by per capita Gross National Product or any other acceptable indicator. The available data does not either support or refute this hypothesis but from knowledge of domestic water demand, it would seem to be a justifiable one (see Fig. 1). This result is probably a reflection of using crude water consumption data in the figure. The data do not show the type of consumption, domestic, commercial, or industrial, or the extent of distribution losses.[63] Consequently, it does not show real consumption for domestic purposes.

If water supply systems are to obtain the optimum return on the investments made or are to be used as a contributor to economic growth, whatever that contribution may be, the needs for water at different levels of economic development must be understood. The present assumption underlying water supply planning appears to be that development without a water supply system is not possible. The construction of actual supply systems, as in the history of the west, has been largely left as an engineering and financial problem to be solved on the basis of experienced judgment but with little or no economic or social guidance.

It is clearly desirable, therefore, to measure and define the relationship between economic development and the provision or need for public water supply systems. Measures are needed which can give concrete guidance or criteria for decision-making in investment policy and priority planning.

---

[62]Ibid., 28.

[63]In the United States, 16 per cent of the water supply systems show losses of over 20 per cent of the water distributed (H. F. Siedel and E. H. Baumann, "A Statistical Analysis of Water Works Data for 1955," Journal of the American Water Works Association, XLIX, No. 12 [December, 1957], 1537).

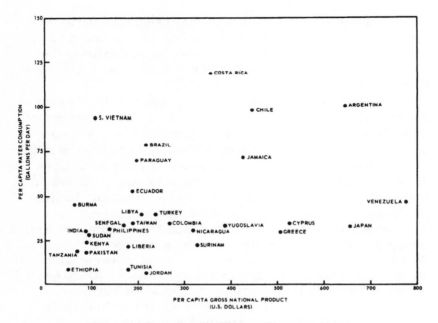

Fig. 1. Per Capita Water Consumption
and Per Capita Income

SOURCES: a. <u>Water Consumption.</u> — Bernd H. Dieterich and John M. Henderson, <u>Urban Water Supply Conditions and Needs in Seventy-Five Developing Countries,</u> World Health Organization Public Health Paper No. 23 (Geneva: WHO, 1963); United Nations, <u>Water Desalination in Developing Countries</u> (New York: UN, 1964); United States, State Department, "Report of the Panel of Expert Consultants to the International Cooperation Administration . . . ," April, 1960 (mimeographed); World Bank; World Health Organization.

        b. <u>Gross National Product.</u> —International Bank for Reconstruction and Development, <u>World Bank Atlas of Per Capita Product and Population</u> (Washington, D.C.: World Bank, 1966).

If a relationship between water demand and socio-economic differences could be established, it would greatly simplify the planning of supply systems in developing countries. The provision of water supply would be tied to other elements in the development process. A necessary task seems to be the exploration of existing water consumption patterns. An understanding of present variations in domestic consumption would be the foundation upon which to build the prediction of future patterns of demand. Such prediction is necessary if the systems are to be designed in a more optimal fashion.

A Theoretical Relationship between Water Needs
and the Level of Economic Development

The existing policy towards the provision of water supply
systems falls well short of the policy recommended here.
There is a strong argument for minimizing investment in social
overhead facilities, including water supply. Present policy does
not achieve this. In the absence of general criteria for decision-
making, the development of a truly rational policy is not possible. Even with the increasing emphasis on the commercial
operation of water supply systems, an optimum solution will
not be generated unless decision-making is placed in a broader
framework. The requirements of social policy are not only
that the project may be self-supporting, but that it produces the
best return or highest benefits on the particular investment.
There is a need for a more rigorous appraisal of actual demands
for water.

It is suggested here that the optimum size of water supply
systems at different levels of development would follow the path
shown by the shape of the theoretical curve (Fig. 2). The relationship shown is a very simplified one—the levels of per capita
needs at different levels of per capita Gross National Product.
The latter is used as representative of the level of economic
development.[64]

The theoretical curve shown in Fig. 2 was based on three
assumptions concerning the nature of the relationships between
economic development and water supply:

(1) There is a certain basic level of supply essential for
public health reasons, for sustained economic and urban growth.
At this level (part A of the theoretical curve), it can be hypothesized that the lack of a public water supply inhibits growth.

(2) Once this basic supply has been ensured, the ability to
supply increased amounts of water per capita is by definition no
longer necessary for health or economic and urban growth. It
is suggested that investment in increased water supply should
be reduced to a level consistent with the maintenance of these
minimal standards. The amount of water required is likely to

---

[64]There is a considerable disagreement in the literature over the most relevant
measurement for levels of economic development. A wider discussion of the various
measures does not seem pertinent here. A discussion of the various measures is
given in D. C. McClelland, "Does Education Contribute to Economic Growth?"
Economic Development and Cultural Change, XIV, No. 3 (April, 1963), 260-261.

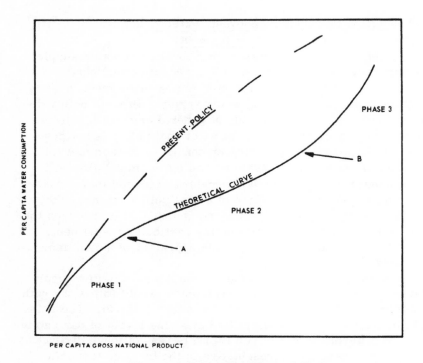

Fig. 2. Water Supply and Economic Development

be low and a higher level of supply can be regarded as serving
non-essential uses.

(3) In both parts B and C of the curve, urban water supply
can be used as a device to encourage growth in line with national
development goals. The relationship between urban water supply
and economic development can be used to formulate a policy in
regard to the provision, organization, and pricing of water which
will bring the greatest constructive benefits for economic development at least cost.

The existing situation varies from the theoretical curve in
the critical second stage of the development process, independent of the form the stage may actually take.[65] There is a tend-

---

[65]The use of the word stage here is not meant to suggest the stages of economic
development as defined by Rostow.

ency to supply more water per capita and to build larger systems than is suggested by the present analysis. The higher levels of supply that are provided under current policies, particularly a tendency to plan in terms of complete house connections to the system, give few benefits and the larger investment in water supply would be better employed elsewhere.

In chapters iii and iv, an attempt is made to establish the actual form of the lower levels of the theoretical curve on the basis of case studies made in Calcutta and New Delhi. The study provides also an insight into the strength of the relationship between the consumption of water and selected social and economic variables. It can be viewed as an investigation of the demand relationships and the demand curve for water under conditions of economic growth and social change.

CHAPTER II

A GEOGRAPHIC APPROACH TO THE DELIMITATION
OF PATTERNS OF WATER CONSUMPTION

In order to investigate the problems outlined in chapter i, a study of domestic water consumption and patterns of water use was designed. The fieldwork was conducted in India during 1965 and 1966 and concentrated mainly in Calcutta and New Delhi. The study was undertaken in a number of different living environments in each city. A basic premise is that an understanding of the role of water supply in the development process can only be gained through the inventory, examination, and analysis of the demand for water. An attempt is made to establish the present form of water-use activities and to relate the present form to the planning of the future provision of water supply.

An inquiry is also made into the relationship between the existing level of water consumption and the hypothetical curve outlined in the previous chapter. Data are presented as an empirical test of the underlying assumptions about the nature of water use and the demand for water used in the construction of the hypothetical curve.

Water Supply and Urbanization

It is hypothesized that there is an ecological relationship between water use and the living environment, a relationship identified by the influence of this environment on the level of water consumption in the household and the habits of water use. Households in similar living environments, therefore, will have similar levels of consumption and water-use habits. A type of relationship producing a wide variation is the level of water consumption in the city in an underdeveloped country. The city is never a homogeneous unit and in the underdeveloped economy variations and differences in the urban environment are far

greater than in the cities of the west.[1] The nature of the urban
society plays an important part in limiting the levels of water
consumption. The dichotomy, in water consumption, between
those households with a private water connection and those without, is a reflection of a more general pattern found in the demand for urban social overhead facilities. The social and
economic character of the city shown in its physical morphology
is reflected in differences in domestic water consumption and
patterns of water use.

If differences in water consumption are related to variations
in the living environment, it is necessary to consider what type
of living environments are found in a city and their distribution,
if the optimum planning of water supply systems is to be achieved.
It is necessary to understand that the population will place differing demands on the water supply system according to the nature of the way in which they use water. If these demands can
be generalized according to different living or residential environments, then an understanding of the urban structure is important in improving the planning of water supply systems. It
would allow for the more detailed and accurate prediction of per
capita demands. The level of demand would depend upon the
types of housing or living environments found in the city, particularly the rate of growth of individual house connections to the
water supply system.

Urban Structure and Water Use

The level of per capita demand used for the design of a
particular water-use system will depend on the urban structure
of the city for which the system is to be built. There are, however, certain general features of the social and economic characteristics of the Indian city which are especially significant to
the planning of water supply systems. The contemporary Indian
city is characterized by a chaotic mixture of land uses and a
great range in housing types and living conditions. Important
aspects of the morphology of the city or the form of urbanization
are crucial to the delineating of demands for water supply and
other social overhead services. Social and economic characteris-

---

[1]Nirmal K. Bose, "Calcutta: A Premature Metropolis," Scientific American,
CCXIII, No. 3 (September, 1965), 91-102.

tics and morphology are closely related. The form of the city
will be discussed first and then related to certain socio-economic
characteristics.

The outstanding feature of the morphology of the city is the
high proportion of slum areas containing shack or bustee type
housing. In most cities this is the most obvious, but not the
sole, rift in the urban structure in that there is a separation
between these areas and the rest of the city. Functionally, all
the various parts of the city are linked at one level or another
at least by interdependence within the urban economic system.
In other respects, the city is a complex of discrete units; not
merely the shacks or bustees against the permanent housing,
but between the different income, social, and cultural groups
which together make up the city. The bustee dweller's city is
a much different entity compared to that of the business executive. There is a lack of centralizing influences in the city and
the poor tend to live entirely in one locality, whereas the rich
may live in commuter suburbs and use the Anglicized business
and entertainment facilities in the city centre. The different
commercial areas in an Indian city tend to complement and
supplement each other rather than to compete with each other.[2]
The pattern of business areas is a reflection of the local units
within which most of the urban population live.

The slum areas tend, themselves, to be self contained,
with their own workshops, bazaars, and other retail outlets
and similar functions. Traditional studies of urban morphology
and structure have tended to ignore or pass over the function
and place of the slum or bustee accretion in the city. They are
commonly treated as not being "true Residential quarters" of
the city.[3] In much of the literature, especially in the Indian
journals, the slum is treated as something extraneous which
will go away if ignored or can be relatively easily removed by
a minor adjustment in social and economic policies. The existing models of urban form used to explain the structure of the
city do not take account of the slum phenomena or the social
and cultural diversity of the Indian city, a diversity which is a

[2]See J. E. Brush, "The Morphology of Indian Cities," in India's Urban Future, ed.
by R. Turner, pp. 67-70.

[3]See for example, M. Guha and A. B. Chatterjee, "Serampore—A Study in Urban
Geography," Geographical Review of India, XVI, No. 4 (December, 1954), 38-44.

dominant characteristic of the city:

> The map of Calcutta . . . shows a highly differen-
> tiated texture. Ethnic groups tend to cluster together
> in their own quarters. They are distinguished from
> one another not only by language and culture but also
> by broad differences in the way they make their liv-
> ing. Naturally there is a considerable amount of
> overlap, but this does not obscure the fact that each
> ethnic group tends to pursue a particular range of
> occupations. [4]

Calcutta and other cities are, as Bose notes, fragmented
socially into units divided by caste, class, and occupations.
The class distinctions are growing more significant at the ex-
pense of caste. Differences of class are reflected in terms of
differences in the quality of the residential or living environment. The nature of the living environment is determined by
the class or economic position of the residents of any particular part of the city.

The social fragmentation of the city is undeniably important particularly in attempts to bring about cultural change.
But it is only part of the fragmentation of the urban structure.
Economic fragmentation has even greater significance here.
This is especially true in the consideration of the planning of
the provision of individual parts of the social infrastructure system required to support economic growth. The structural fragmentation of the city is important to system design but it is a
factor which has been little considered.

Urban Morphology and Ecology

There have been a considerable number of studies of the
urban structure and the urban geography of Indian cities. [5]
Most of these studies have been made within India. In addition,

---

[4]Bose, "Calcutta: A Premature Metropolis," 102.

[5]An impression of the extent of the literature can be gained from S. P. Chatterjee's
account of Indian geography in the last fifty years (Fifty Years of Science in India;
Progress of Geography, pp. 193-208 and pp. 215-218). Examples include: P. Rao,
Towns of Mysore State, pp. 62-74; R. L. Singh, Bangalore: An Urban Survey; Ujagir
Singh, Allahabad: A Study in Urban Geography.

more recently, a large-scale attempt has been made to survey the conditions of life in all the larger urban areas.[6]

The morphological and ecological studies seem largely to have come to the conclusion that the urban structure of Indian cities, in agreement with experience in other underdeveloped countries, is very different from that of the western city.[7] Where strict comparisons have been made, as in Gist's study of Bangalore,[8] the major distinction emphasized is the diffuse structure of the Indian city compared to the more clearly differentiated nature of its western counterpart. Brush comments that "centrifugal forces are relatively weak" in Indian cities and that in rapidly growing centres increasing overcrowding is very common.[9] Berry similarly found that in applying Clark's density gradients to Indian cities there was a tendency for the gradients to remain the same or even increase rather than decrease over time.[10]

The less definite structure of the Indian city produced by the complexity of land use is accompanied by much higher densities of development than in the city of the west. The urban facilities tend to be provided at different levels for the various sectors of the population. The provision of services for the westernized upper classes is placed upon the patterns of the almost feudal city of the mass of the population. The poor tend to live near their place of work and consumer services are provided on a local basis. This has led to intense congestion of development and a tendency for the city not to throw out suburban accretions as in the west. The city is at least because of this, a dual entity.

The distinction between these two groups of the population is not made clear in the morphological and ecological studies of Indian cities. It is noted in some, as in Learmonth's descriptions of Bangalore:

---

[6]Much of this work is summarized in Jal F. Bulsara, Problems of Rapid Urbanization in India.

[7]N. P. Gist, "The Ecological Structure of an Asian City: An East-West Comparison," Population Review, II, No. 1 (January, 1958), 17.

[8]Ibid., 25

[9]Brush, "The Morphology of Indian Cities," p. 69.

[10]Brian J. L. Berry, James W. Simmons, and Robert J. Tennant, "Urban Population Densities: Structure and Change," Geographical Review, LIII, No. 3 (July, 1963), 389-405.

New Townscapes of factory and associated town-
ships with houses for different grades of employees
have been added to the old dichotomy of fort and old
city on the one hand and cantonment on the other.
Well-to-do houses, . . . spread along the gneissic
ridges, while the ill-drained hollows are filled with
more modest dwellings or at worst with rather mo-
bile and transient yet persistently recurring slums
of mud, flattened kerosene tins and palm thatch.[11]

The nature of the structure of the Indian city and of the conditions of life is more apparent from the socio-economic surveys produced in recent years under the auspices of the Planning
Commission. These studies present description and detailed
statistics for a number of Indian cities. From them a more detailed account of the types of living environments common in the
city can be constructed.

The Socio-Economic Nature of the City

The socio-economic studies of Indian cities have been concerned with a far wider range of the problems of urbanization
than is the concern here. Among the many aspects of urban
life surveyed was the physical nature of the urban environment—
housing, municipal services, and other urban facilities particularly. The information from these surveys discussed here will
be supplemented by more detailed data for Calcutta.

The viewpoint of the surveys is very different from that
gained from the morphological studies. The major emphasis
in the surveys is placed upon the lack of the basic requirements
of urban living among the overwhelming proportion of the urban
population (Table 7).[12]

The impression given by all these reports, without exception, is of the appalling living conditions found in most Indian
cities. There is a tendency for the conditions to be somewhat

---

[11] A. T. A. Learmonth, "Retrospect on a Project in Applied Regional Geography,
Mysore State, India," in Geographers and the Tropics: Liverpool Essays, ed. by R.
W. Steele and R. Mansell Prothero, pp. 343-344.

[12] The surveys discussed here cover eleven cities: Baroda, Bombay, Calcutta,
Gorakhpur, Hubli, Hyderabad-Secunderabad, Jamshedpur, Kanpur, Lucknow, Poona,
and Surat.

TABLE 7   THE LACK OF URBAN AMENITIES
IN THE INDIAN CITY

| City | Percentage of the Population with | | | | |
	2 or less Rooms	No Independent Water Tap	No Latrine Facilities	No Separate Kitchen	No Electricity
Baroda	-[a]	-	-	64.3	47.3
Bombay	91.7	72.0	87.3	71.4	41.2
Calcutta[b]	78.2	73.0	87.2	77.0	49.0
Gorakhpur	48.0[c]	66.5	59.3	54.6	91.8
Hubli	63.2	87.6	86.6	43.0	-
Hyderabad-Secunderabad	52.0	-	-	-	68.3
Jamshedpur	-	74.5	52.8	-	50.1
Kanpur	86.8	87.2	-	-	62.0
Lucknow	75.2	64.6	49.8	63.1	81.7
Poona	79.9	66.7	87.0	-	-
Surat	60.0	54.0	67.0	-	-

[a]No data.

[b]S. N. Sen, The City of Calcutta: A Socio-Economic Survey, 1954-55 to 1957-58 (Calcutta: Bookland Private, 1960).

[c]One room or less.

SOURCE: Jal F. Bulsara, Problems of Rapid Urbanization in India (Bombay: Popular Prakashan, 1964).

better in the smaller cities but the differences are not great. Even in the smaller cities overcrowding is very common and only a small proportion of the population live in anything but extreme discomfort. In the typical urban household "the living room, bedroom, kitchen, and bathroom are all in a single room . . . where there is no extra space available for cooking and bathroom."[13]

Overcrowding may be less severe in the smaller cities but certain amenities, particularly electricity, are more widely available in the largest cities. It would be difficult to balance the two factors against each other.

In contrast to the vast majority of the population, there is a proportion of households in all these cities which are relatively well provided with the amenities of urban life. These households tend to be those in the highest income groups, although they would also include that section of the population in

---

[13]Bulsara, Problems of Rapid Urbanization, p. 64.

44

government or privately provided "model" housing. The better housing tends to form a distinct element in the urban structure, although it is found in juxtaposition with the bulk of poor housing. Even in the bustees there are isolated middle class houses.

The more detailed information contained in the survey of Calcutta allows identification of this better-served section of the population. In the survey these households are classified as those families living in a separate house or flat of permanent construction. The households in this group are characterized by a generally high level of income and, associated with this, a high standard of living; but this accounts for only 7.5 per cent of the total number of households and 17.5 per cent of the multi-member households.

There are considerable differences between the level of the standard of living or the living environment of this group and the remainder, as indicated in Tables 7 and 8. The contrast would probably be less sharp if differences in family size were taken into account. The situation is also marginally modified by the existence, on a limited scale, of standardized low-cost housing, housing still overcrowded but with the essential basic amenities, including water supply, a kitchen, and a bathroom. [14]

The Urban Environment in Calcutta

A mixture of land uses, the hodge-podge and complex nature of the urban structure typical of Indian cities, reaches its climax in Calcutta,

> The most characteristic feature of the city's housing
> is that on a large number of roads, one will find a
> few houses, often palatial buildings just by the side
> of which there is one of these abominable bustees.
> One finds quite a number of fashionable houses in
> coexistence in different parts of the city. [15]

---

[14] There are numerous reports on different types and standards of low-cost housing. Typical examples of this accommodation can be found in the two reports cited here: India, Ministry of Labour, Low-Cost Housing for Industrial Workers; India, Planning Commission, Committee on Plan Projects, Building Projects Team, Report on Residential Buildings.

[15] S. N. Sen, The City of Calcutta: A Socio-Economic Survey, 1954-55 to 1957-58, p. 161.

TABLE 8   CALCUTTA HOUSEHOLDS,
LIVING CONDITIONS, 1954-58

Characteristic	Percentage of Households	
	Separate Houses or Flats	All Households
Houses with electric light	96.0	51.0
Houses with one or more taps	95.7	9.2
Houses with one or more lavatories	97.0	10.3
Houses with a separate kitchen	61.4 (90.4)*	23.0

*Bracketed percentage refers to separate flats.

SOURCE: S. N. Sen, The City of Calcutta (Calcutta: Bookland Private, 1960), pp. 122-163.

TABLE 9   CALCUTTA HOUSEHOLDS, LEVELS OF
FAMILY INCOME, 1954-58

Monthly Income (Rupees)	Percentage of Households	
	Separate Houses or Flats	All other Households
less than 200	1.0	99.0
201 - 350	29.0	71.0
over 350	64.0	36.0

SOURCE: Sen, The City of Calcutta: A Socio-Economic Survey, pp. 131-132.

Some of the major functions are spatially distinct but this pattern forms merely part of the total structure of the city. In much of the urban area there is no clear distinction between land uses. Residential use, especially the houses of the poor, small commercial enterprises, and even small scale industry, are omnipresent. The West Bengal Legislative Building, for example, is flanked by a bustee. All the main streets carry their quota of "temporary" sidewalk dwellers.

Some generalizations can be made about the distribution of different types of land uses in Calcutta. The central area of the city tends to have a higher proportion of permanent buildings than the peripheries, with the exception of a strip extending into

TABLE 10   RESIDENTIAL DENSITIES IN
THE CITY OF CALCUTTA

Area	Population	Population Density Persons Per Acre		Total
		Bustee	Non-Bustee	
North Calcutta	211,540	217	277	254
North-Central Calcutta	1,053,285	832	597	633
Eastern Suburbs	414,870	242	344	292
South-Central Calcutta	693,530	604	248	274
Southwest Suburbs	270,830	459	94	202
Southeast Suburbs	268,921	-	-	129

SOURCE: Unpublished material in the files of the Calcutta Metropolitan Planning Organization.

the southern suburbs (Fig. 3).[16]   Densities do not follow the
same pattern although there are similarities (Fig. 4, Table 10).
The inter-mixture of land uses is sufficient to obscure any
significant relationship between the proportion of kutcha housing
in a ward and the residential density, the number of persons per
room (r = 0.16).[17]

Despite the higher densities common in the areas of bustees
and their generally low sanitary standards, they can appear at-
tractive features of the urban scene. Not so far beneath the surface, however, they are generally now, as in the past,

> . . . abodes of misery, vice and filth, and the nur-
> series of sickness and disease. In these bustees
> abound green and slimy stagnant ponds, full of pu-
> trid vegetable and animal matter in a state of decom-

[16]Housing in India is normally classified into two types: (1) Kutcha or temporary
construction, usually built with mud and bamboo, although cardboard, tin cans, and
other materials may also be used; (2) Pukka or permanent construction, buildings
made with burnt bricks or concrete, with brick or concrete foundations; some buildings are constructed with materials of both types.

[17]The terms kutcha and bustee are not interchangeable. A bustee is a legally defined type of housing under the Calcutta Municipal Act, 1951. The Municipal Act de-
fines.a bustee as:
> an area containing land occupied by or for the purposes of any col-
> lection of huts standing on a plot not less than 10 kathas [approxi-
> mately one-sixth of an acre] and a hut means any building, no
> substantial part of which, including the walls up to a height of 18
> inches above the floor or floor level, is constructed of masonary,
> reinforced concrete, steel, iron or other metals.

47

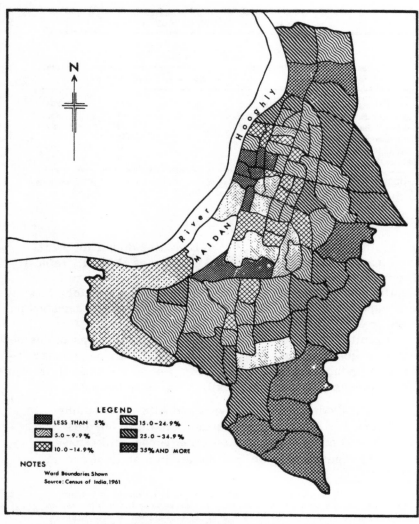

LEGEND

LESS THAN 5%   15.0 - 24.9%

5.0 - 9.9%   25.0 - 34.9%

10.0 - 14.9%   35% AND MORE

NOTES

Ward Boundaries Shown
Source: Census of India, 1961

Fig. 3.   Calcutta: Proportion of Dwellings
with Kutcha Walls, by Ward, 1961

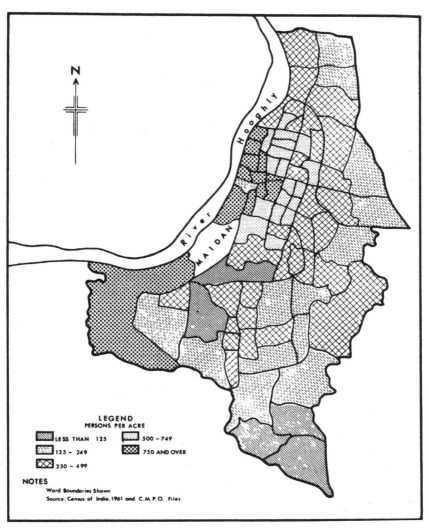

LEGEND
PERSONS PER ACRE

LESS THAN 125
125 – 249
250 – 499
500 – 749
750 AND OVER

NOTES
Ward Boundaries Shown
Source: Census of India, 1961 and C.M.P.O. Files

Fig. 4.   Calcutta: Population Density,
by Ward, 1961

position, whose bubbling surfaces exhale under a
tropical sun noxious gasses poisoning the atmosphere
and spreading around disease and death. [18]

There have been few changes in the quality of the living environment found in the Calcutta bustees during the ninety years
since MacNamara wrote this description.

The outstanding feature of the city in India and the underdeveloped countries generally is the poor quality of the living
environment of most of the population. The poverty of the environment has many facets among which the lack of or deficiencies in water supply is only one.

In India, a raising of the standard of housing to 2.5 persons
per room from the present 2.7 persons would require the construction of 6,150,000 dwelling units in the 10-year period,
1961-1971. [19] The present planned total level of construction
in the public sector is only 2,200,000 units. It is certain that
the private sector cannot make up the deficit. In addition to the
requirements of new housing, there would have to be replace-
ment of existing obsolete buildings. In Calcutta, the situation
is even more critical. The proposed rate of construction in the
whole of the Fourth Five Year Plan period, 1966-1971, is not
sufficient to satisfy the demand generated in one year by population increase alone. [20]

The construction of water supply systems cannot be at an
optimum level unless attention is paid to the actual nature of the
structure of the city and conditions of life. Unfortunately, much
of the prevailing strategy towards the provision of water supply
does not take sufficient cognizance of the existing situation. Improvements in housing conditions must be the prerequisite to
any general attempt to raise the level of the urban living environment.

---

[18]C. MacNamara, History of Asiatic Cholera, pp. 415-416.

[19]Leo Jakobson, "A Note on Housing in the Calcutta Metropolitan District." Report
to the Ford Foundation Advisory Planning Group, Calcutta Metropolitan Plan, January
15, 1965, p. 31. (Mimeographed.)

[20]Ibid., pp. 57-58.

The Pattern of Living Environments
and Water Supply Planning

Variations in living conditions in urban areas give rise to considerable differences in the consumption of water. Planning the provision of water supply, therefore, on the assumption of uniform or average levels of consumption could lead to over-investment in the water supply system. The existence of variable demand for water would suggest that in the planning of water supply systems, there is a necessity to isolate those factors which are most significant in the assessment of the need for water supply. It is not meant to suggest that considerations of external factors which may effect levels of water consumption are completely ignored in current water supply planning. There is, however, a need to systematize the nature of the relationships between water consumption, the pattern of water use, and the living environment.

Many of the existing reports and plans for water supply systems in the cities of underdeveloped countries do take cognizance of different levels of consumption produced by differences in living conditions. The most common distinction that is made is between those consumers dependent upon public taps or fountains and those with individual house connections (Table 11).

In reports on two water supply systems in Pakistan, Karachi and Lahore, a more elaborate differentiation of levels of consumption is made. The Karachi report relates water consumption to residential densities. The Lahore report relates water consumption to income levels. The range in the assumed average levels of consumption is from 15 gallons per capita per day with a residential density of over 350 persons per acre to 60 gallons per day in areas where the density is only 10-30 persons per acre in Karachi. The assumed level of consumption in Lahore varies from 25 gallons per capita per day in households with incomes less than 200 rupees a month (US $42.00) to 60 gallons per capita per day with incomes of over 1,000 rupees a month (US $212.00).

In many Latin American cities the assumption that levels of water consumption will rise with higher socio-economic status is reflected in the use of income levels or housing types as the basis of the water charges tariff. The water tariff in Barranquila, Columbia, allows for different water rates ac-

51

City	Conditions of Consumption	Level of Consumption (Gallons Per Day)
Accra-Tema, Ghana[a]	House Connection	40.0
	Fountain	12.7
Adala, Turkey[a]	Good Housing	23.3
	Poor Housing	11.0-15.7
	Fountain	6.6
Ville de Cotoneau, Dahomey[a]	House Connection	55.0
	Fountain	1.4
Saigon, S. Vietnam[b]	House Connection	93.0
	Fountain	11.0
Chittagong, Pakistan[c]	House Connection	15.6-37.0
	Fountain	2.5
Dacca, Pakistan[c]	House Connection	16.9-60.0
	Fountain	2.5
Bangalore, India[c]	Upper-income Housing	40.0
	Average Housing	10.0-15.0
Yaounde, Cameroun[d]	House Connection	44.0
	Fountain	4.2
Douala, Cameroun[d]	House Connection	46.2
	Fountain	4.0

[a]SOURCE: Files of the World Health Organization, Geneva, Switzerland.

[b]W. T. McPhee, "Water Supply for Saigon," Civil Engineering, XXXV, No. 9 (September, 1965), 59-63.

[c]Files of the International Bank for Reconstruction and Development, Washington, D.C., U.S.A.

[d]Cameroun, Ministère des Travaux Public et des Transports, Direction des Travaux Public, Bulletin Statistique, Production et-Distribution D'Energie Électrique et D'eau Potable, 1963.

cording to the assessed value of the house. Consumers living in houses of the lowest assessed value pay four pesos a month (US $0.56) for a minimum of forty cubic metres of water while the highest value households pay fifteen pesos a month (US $2.12) for a minimum of seventy cubic metres of water.[21] In Mexico City, the rate charged per cubic metre consumed increases with a higher total monthly consumption.[22]

[21]O. Bahamonde, "Estudio de Tarifas de Abastecimento de Agua," Report to the Pan-American Health Organization, 1966, p. 73. (Mimeographed.)

[22]Ibid.

It is widely recognized that the demand for water changes at different levels of economic development. Nyerges suggests three levels of development that are significant from the viewpoint of water supply planning. These are: (1) primitive traditional rural society, (2) developing urban societies which have passed the first stage of the socio-economic revolution, and (3) more mature economies with standards of demand similar to those found in the west.[23]

In a more detailed discussion of the determination of levels of consumption for the purpose of gaining an insight into the demand function for water, Bahamonde suggests a number of factors that may effect demand. These include: (a) demographic and housing variations within the city; (b) the influence of the type of water connection on the level of consumption; (c) the relationship between the amount of water rate and the average water rate; (d) the need to determine the characteristics of consumption by consumer type for sub-areas within the water supply system; and (e) the proportion of buildings without a connection and the reasons for the absence of service.[24]

There is, therefore, a recognition of the importance of the influence of external social and economic factors, the living environment, on the demand for water. Consequently, there is a realization of the need to take account of these factors in the planning of the construction and operation of water supply systems. At the same time, differences in patterns of water use which accompany variations in the living environment found in the city are also important in the demand function. If this knowledge is to be useful to the planning of water supply systems, a careful estimation must be made of the likely demands that the particular system must meet. It is not sufficient to merely make a crude distinction between that part of the population dependent on public taps and that with individual house connections, as is common practice at the present time. Demand estimates derived from partial investigations can be very unreliable and

[23]N. Nyerges, "Social and Economic Considerations Affecting the Development of Design Standards," in Pan-American Health Organization, Proceedings of Seminar on Water System Design (Buenos Aires, September 20-29, 1962), p. 5. (Mimeographed.)

[24]Bahamonde, "The Preparation of Preliminary and Complete Projects for Water Supplies," Proceedings of Seminar on Water System Design (Buenos Aires), pp. 16-20.

detract from the validity of the proposed project. The limitations induced by slenderly based demand estimates are illustrated by the current plans for the improvement in the water supply of Calcutta.

The Calcutta Report

The current plans for the improvement of the water supply of Calcutta do take account of the existence of different levels of consumption with differences in living conditions, particularly access to water supply. It is a simple division of the consumers into two groups:

> Group I. Occupants of dwellings containing a variety of plumbing fixtures. This group will include a range from high class dwellings to public rehousing projects of a type containing multi-storied flats.

> Group II. Occupants of dwelling units containing a minimum of plumbing fixtures. The range is from buildings containing one tap and toilet each to buildings where occupants rely on communal plumbing fixtures located outside the building. [25]

The design standards adopted for the two groups are 40 gallons per capita per day for Group I consumers and 20 gallons per capita per day for Group II consumers. Two planning periods were used in the report, the first ending in 1981 and the second in 2001. It was assumed that by 2001 Group I consumers would require a per capita supply of 50 rather than 40 gallons per capita except in the central cities of Calcutta and Howrah where the requirement would be 60 gallons per capita.

The demand figures for Group I consumers were derived from field metering studies in three areas including Kalyani, one of the areas used as a case study here. [26] There is no information in the report on the derivation of the demand figure for the Group II consumers.

---

[25]Calcutta Metropolitan Planning Organization, Survey of Water Supply Resources of Greater Calcutta, Master Plan for Water Supply, Sewerage and Drainage, Calcutta Metropolitan District, 1966-2001, I, Detailed Report prepared for the World Health Organization by Metcalfe and Eddy Ltd. and Engineering Sciences Inc., August, 1966, p. 4-1.

[26]Ibid., p. 3-4.

TABLE 12   HOUSING CONDITIONS, CALCUTTA
METROPOLITAN DISTRICT 1961

Municipality	Population	Proportion of Kutcha Housing*	Proportion of Single-Room Households
Kanchrapara	68,966	26.0	63.3
Halisahar	51,423	33.6	80.5
Naihati	58,457	33.5	74.9
Bhatpara	147,630	8.7	84.2
N. Barrackpur	56,683	18.4	66.8
Titagar	76,429	40.9	93.4
Barrackpur	63,778	27.3	66.9
Panihati	93,749	32.4	65.5
Baranagar	107,837	29.3	62.9
Kamarhati	125,457	33.8	69.6
S. Dum Dum	111,284	48.9	69.7
S. Suburban	185,811	36.2	60.2
Garden Reach	130,770	16.2	81.4
Calcutta	2,927,289	20.4	71.9
Bally	130,896	28.3	77.0
Howrah	512,598	46.0	75.2
Hooghly-Chinsurah	83,104	15.2	50.6
Chandernagore	67,105	29.8	58.7
Serampore	91,521	25.0	71.7

*Houses constructed of grass, leaves, reeds, bamboo, timber, mud or unburnt bricks.

SOURCE: India, Census of India, 1961.

The validity of the adopted demand estimates will be discussed later.   At the present time, criticism will be directed at the anticipated proportions of the two groups of consumers in the two planning periods.   Specific attention will be placed on the predictions for 1981.

The report assumes that by 1981, in all the developed areas of the metropolitan district, two-thirds of the consumers will be in Group I.   This assumption requires that in fifteen years, two-thirds of the population in the urbanized areas will live in good quality housing.[27]   This is a very favourable assessment of the rate of improvement of the housing situation in Calcutta, given the present level of housing quality (Table 12). In none of the larger towns of the Calcutta Metropolitan District do more than half of the population live in houses with more than

---

[27]Ibid.

one room; in many it is less than a quarter. As has been discussed earlier, current plans for housing investment fall well short of the anticipated demands. It would be optimistic to assume that, unless there is a considerable change in housing policy, the situation will improve. There is a far greater probability that the housing situation will deteriorate.

The per capita demand design estimate is the basic piece of data upon which the proposed water supply system rests. The projected increase in demand is related in the report itself to a widespread improvement in living conditions in the Calcutta Metropolitan District. The assumed rate of increase in the number of households with a variety of plumbing fixtures does not represent an objective assessment of the housing situation in Calcutta. It would seem reasonable to question the estimate of water needs on this ground alone, without further examination of the adopted demand figures.

Outline of Case Studies and Methods

The emphasis of the study of domestic water consumption is placed on the two extremes of the existing demand situation: (1) consumers dependent upon public water sources and living in poor housing—the shack development characteristic of the urban environment in the underdeveloped city, and (2) consumers living in good housing with individual house connections for water and a variety of plumbing fixtures.

These parts of the existing demand situation were chosen for study on the assumption that they would provide insight into the most significant questions of concern for planning supply systems. It would provide an understanding of the demand function for water at the lowest level of consumption and provide for a comparison between the two situations. At the same time, it is important to know more of the likely demands in those households living in conditions which may become general as the development process proceeds. Water use and consumption have been studied, therefore, in a number of areas ranging from bustees to high income residential areas with standards of housing and general urban services comparable to the west.

Water consumption and use. —The concern of the study is with the consumer aspects of public water supply. The emphasis is placed upon water consumption and use. These terms are defined for the purposes of this study in a specific manner.

Residential Water Consumption was taken to be the water used in a household for drinking, cooking, bathing, washing clothes and similar purposes, together with the water used for garden irrigation and for cattle watering and washing where appropriate.

Pattern of Water Use is the water-using habits of the household. It includes such factors as the average daily number of baths, the extent to which clothes were washed in the house, and the amount of garden irrigation.

The case studies. —The thirteen case studies undertaken are divided into two major groups (Table 13). The first consists of the studies made of areas of metered house connections in Kalyani and New Delhi. The second encompasses the bustee surveys and source surveys undertaken in Calcutta. The bustee survey was divided into six separate studies of individual bustees located in different parts of Calcutta, including one bustee in Howrah, on the west bank of the River Hooghly. The source surveys were conducted at a large number of different locations within the area of the municipality of Calcutta.

The determining factor in the choice of case study areas was the necessity to measure the consumption of water. This was crucial with the studies of households with individual house connections. The need to measure the water consumption restricted the choice of areas to water supply systems where water was sold through meters. The metering of water supplies is not widespread in West Bengal. The only successful system is in the northern Calcutta suburb of Kalyani. This town was used for one of the case studies. The lack of other areas with metering adjacent to Calcutta led to the decision to use New Delhi for the other-case study of households possessing a variety of plumbing fixtures.

It proved very difficult to undertake a systematic sampling procedure to choose the sample populations in both Kalyani and New Delhi. In Kalyani, water consumption data was obtained for all the households served by the water supply system from the files of the Kancharapara Development Agency. This agency acts as the local municipal authority. It was originally intended that a sample of householders would be interviewed to obtain the necessary socio-economic and water-use information. This approach proved to be impractical due to the absence of the male

TABLE 13 CASE STUDIES CLASSIFIED
BY TYPE OF SUPPLY

Area	Number of Interviews Obtained	Type of Supply	Type of Interview
Metered House Connections			
Kalyani	165	Piped	Mail
New Delhi	436	Piped·	Mail
Public Sources			
Topsia	36	Standpipe Pump Tank	Personal Interview
Goabagan	21	Standpipe Pump Unfiltered hydrant	Personal Interview
Tollygunge	42	Standpipe Pump Tank Unfiltered hydrant Canal	Personal Interview
Beniapukur	50	Standpipe Pump Unfiltered hydrant	Personal Interview
Saheb Bagan	67	Standpipe Pump Unfiltered hydrant Canal	Personal Interview
Pilkhana (Howrah)	62	Standpipe Pump Tank	Personal Interview
TOTAL Calcutta Bustees	278		

Source Surveys			Personal Interview
Standpipe	98		
Pump	118		
Tank	59		
Unfiltered hydrant	16		
Hooghly	49		
TOTAL Source Surveys	340		

members of the household during the day and the reluctance of
women to answer questions posed by our door to door inter –

viewer, however authorized. Instead, a mailed questionnaire was sent to every household. The questionnaire was prepared in both English and Bengali. Some houses were rejected from the survey as they were being used as offices or hostels and houses where the meters were not functioning. Approximately one-third of the households sampled replied to the questionnaire.

In New Delhi the meter readings of water consumption were obtained from the files of the New Delhi Municipal Committee. There are some 60,000 individual house connections to the New Delhi water supply system so that it was not practical to attempt a complete survey. A population of approximately 1400 households was used as the basis of the survey. Sampling again proved a problem as the consumption data could only be taken from the record books used by the billing clerks. These books were in continuous use and so any form of random sampling procedure was not possible. The only sampling method that could be used was to take a representative number of books from the different parts of the city. The Municipal Committee classifies the households into a number of economic groups corresponding to the pay scales of the Union Government. An attempt was made to ensure that sufficient numbers of households were represented in the sample from all groups. The questionnaire was prepared in English and Hindi. Again, approximately one-third of the questionnaires mailed out were returned in a sufficiently complete form to use.

Using a sampling technique of this type allows very little control over the replies received or the final structure of the sample population. Allowing the sample to select itself is liable to introduce bias into the sample obtained and make the sample unrepresentative of the population from which it is taken. Despite these limitations on the techniques used in the study, it is not felt that they place any severe restraints on the results obtained. There are no significant differences between the total consumption of water of the households which replied to the questionnaire compared to those who did not do so in either Kalyani or New Delhi.

The consumption data that was used in both cases covered a number of months. The meter readings were taken quarterly in Kalyani and monthly in New Delhi. It was not possible to use the same period for both studies as data for 1964 was not available in New Delhi. The same months were used for the consumption data in both studies, the months after the cessation of the monsoon. In Kalyani, the consumption figures obtained for this period of 1964 were compared with an annual average figure for 1963; there was no significant difference. There was also no noticeable seasonal variation in average daily per capita water consumption.

In the bustee part of the study, a different technique was used. The water consumption of the household was taken to be that water actually used in the house and fetched from one of the public sources. The measurement of consumption was derived from the capacity of the vessel used to collect water and the number of times a day that water was collected.

The measurement was obtained by measuring the height and circumference, at the widest part, of the vessel used to collect water. These two measurements were then converted into an estimate of the capacity of the vessel. The vessels used were of various shapes and sizes and a means had to be found and empirically developed to allow a minimum of measurements for the calculation of capacity. In order to derive the vessel capacities, fourteen vessels (clay pots and buckets) were measured. The capacity was calculated from the height and circumference and the actual capacity measured. The two capacities were compared and a regression line fitted in order to produce a best estimate for the rapid calculation of the actual capacity from the height and circumference measurements.

It is possible that error was introduced into the capacity measurements in two ways: (1) the nature of the method used to calculate the capacity of the vessel which could only produce an approximate estimate of the size; and (2) in the field the interviewers were not permitted to handle the vessel in some cases so that the measurement was made by the interviewees.

The bustee sample was chosen to give a variety of situations in the occurrence of the different public water sources. The sources available for use by the population dependent on water collected from outside the house include:
1. The standpipe or public tap connected to the filtered water supply system.
2. The tubewell or handpump supplying groundwater.
3. The tank, an artificial pond very commonly found in Calcutta.
4. The unfiltered water hydrant, a ground-level water

hydrant connected to the unfiltered water system.

    5.   Water from surface streams and drainage canals including the River Hooghly.

All the water used for domestic consumption was not taken to the house. A number of water-use activities were undertaken at the source. If the water was used at the source it was not possible to measure the amount consumed. Instead, use at the source was used as a variable expected to reduce the level of daily water consumption.

An important part of the pattern of water use in areas with dependence on public sources of supply is the use of unsafe sources of water. In Calcutta, the sources generally considered to be unsafe are the tanks, the unfiltered hydrants, and the river.[28] It is necessary to know the role that these sources play in the water consumption pattern if danger from waterborne disease is to be eliminated or lessened. In order to know more of the purposes for which the different sources were used, the household interviews were supplemented by interviews conducted at the sources.

The bustee case study areas were chosen from air photographs in order to provide examples of differing supply situations. It was necessary to identify the bustees in the field. The choice of the sample within the bustees was selected on the basis of obtaining a representation of households with different available complexes of water sources. The bustee is a heterogeneous collection of huts which cannot be identified individually in any way to allow the taking of a systematic sample. Each bustee normally possesses a number of street addresses but these refer to the landholdings not the huts and are very difficult to identify in the field. In these circumstances it appeared to be preferable to control the sample taken as strictly as possible rather than to attempt any form of independent selection.

The household information and water-use measurements were collected by personal interviews conducted by field investigators of the Calcutta Metropolitan Planning Organization

---

[28] See the following for an account of attempts to link the use of these sources for water and the occurrence of cholera and other waterborne diseases: Abou-Gareeb, "The Detection of Cholera Endemic Centres in Calcutta City," 343-353; idem, "The Detection of Cholera Vibrios in Calcutta Waters: The River Hooghly and Canals," Journal of Hygiene, LVIII (1960), 21-33; idem, "The Detection of Cholera Vibrios in Calcutta Waters: The Tanks and Dhobas," 65-66.

(see Appendix A). The household interview information was extended by a number of interviews of water uses at the sources. The areas chosen for the source interviews were selected by dividing the City of Calcutta into a grid and choosing squares within the grid from a table of random numbers. The information obtained in this part of the study was restricted to the purposes for which the water from the source was used, the extent of the use of the source, and the distance over which the user had travelled to reach the source.

The socio-economic information obtained from the bustee studies was compared to that obtained in other investigations of the bustee population. A comparison of the income distribution of the sample population with that of the whole of the bustee population given in the Bustee Survey of the West Bengal State Statistical Bureau shows some differences but an overall similarity (Table 14). The differences that do occur may result from the 10-year lag in the collection of the information and the deliberate attempt to keep higher income bustee families (with individual house connections to the water supply system) out of the sample used in this study.

A further comparison of the results obtained in the bustee case study was obtained from a comparison of the uses made of the different sources with data from a survey carried out by the Cholera Research Centre of the Indian Council of Medical Research.[29] This information was obtained as part of a number of Cholera Carrier Studies being pursued by the Cholera Research Centre under the auspices of the West Bengal Government and the World Health Organization. The distribution of the purposes for which the sources are used shows a similar predominance of the standpipe and pump for all purposes but most markedly as a source of water for drinking (Table 15).
Distances were also measured in the Cholera Carrier Survey but it is difficult to compare the results, as distances travelled vary greatly from bustee to bustee according to the number of available sources for water supply. The distribution of households according to the distance travelled to fetch water in the two surveys do show a number of similarities.

---

[29]I am indebted to Dr. D. L. Shrivastava, Director, Cholera Research Centre for the use of this information.

TABLE 14 BUSTEE INCOME DISTRIBUTION

Monthly Family Income (Rupees)	Present Sample 1965-1966	Bustee Survey* 1958-1959
less than 50	5.9	16.7
51 - 100	49.5	50.0
101 - 150	32.6	17.8
151 - 200	8.7	7.5
201 and over	3.3	7.0

SOURCE: West Bengal, State Statistical Bureau, "Report of the Bustee Survey in Calcutta, 1958-1959," Consolidated Report, XVII (unpublished), p. 12.

TABLE 15 USE OF WATER SOURCES, BY PURPOSE

Purpose	Cholera Carrier Survey[a]		Bustee Survey		Source Survey	
	Number	Per Cent	Number	Per Cent	Number	Per Cent
Drinking						
Standpipe and pump	359	99.5	278	100.0	287	98.6
Other[b]	2	0.5	-	-	4	1.4
Bathing						
Standpipe and pump	260	71.8	260	93.5	114	49.0
Other[b]	101	28.2	18	6.5	6.5	51.0

[a]SOURCE: Letter from Dr. D. L. Shrivastava, Director, Cholera Research Centre, Calcutta, 28 June, 1966.

[b]Sources included under this heading are tanks, open wells, unfiltered water hydrants, and surface streams.

The following two chapters present the results obtained from these case studies and the analysis of the results. A correlation analysis is performed relating variations in water consumption to the socio-economic characteristics of the population and more broadly to differences in the living environment. Water-use habits are also introduced into the analysis and examined in relationship to variations in the nature of the living environment.

CHAPTER III

PATTERNS OF WATER USE AND CONSUMPTION
—METERED AREAS

This chapter and the following chapter describe those areas in
which the studies of water use and consumption were made. It
consists of a delineation of the water use and water consumption characteristics and the general socio-economic character
of the populations surveyed. This information was analyzed by
means of multiple correlation and regression to determine to
what extent the level of water consumption is dependent upon
or can be explained by the selected variables.

The metered areas are most obviously distinguished by the
general high standard of the living environment, including the
provision of individual house connections for water. An important difference between the supply of water in Kalyani and New
Delhi is the existence of a continuous supply in the former and
a discontinuous supply in the latter. It has been observed that
interruptions in the supply of water tend to increase rather than
decrease gross consumption. Discontinuities in supply lead to
storage in the house which may encourage waste. The possibility of this in New Delhi is reduced by the presence of storage
tanks in the household plumbing system. Few respondents were
aware that the supply was not continuous. Climatic differences
can also affect the level of water consumption, particularly
through the amount of garden irrigation. The monsoon rainfall
is heavier and lasts longer in Calcutta (Table 16). It might be
expected that more garden irrigation would be found in New
Delhi, but the New Delhi sample includes large numbers of
apartment dwellers. It is unlikely, therefore, that the rainfall
differential is of importance.

TABLE 16 CLIMATIC STATISTICS, NEW DELHI AND CALCUTTA

Place	Average Annual	January	February	March	April	May	June	July	August	September	October	November	December
Temperature													
New Delhi[a]	77°	57	62	72	82	92	92	88	86	84	79	68	59
Calcutta[b]	79°	67	71	81	86	86	85	83	83	84	81	74	67
Rainfall (inches)													
New Delhi	25.2 in.	0.9	0.7	0.5	0.3	0.5	2.9	7.1	6.8	4.6	0.4	0.1	0.4
Calcutta	63.0 in.	0.4	1.2	1.4	1.7	5.5	11.7	12.8	12.9	9.9	4.5	0.8	0.2

[a]Altitude = 714 feet.

[b]Altitude = 25 feet.

SOURCE: W. G. Kendrew, Climate of the Continents (Oxford: Oxford University Press, 1961).

Kalyani

Water Consumption

The water supply is provided from a number of deep tube-wells with a present pumping capacity of 1.8 million gallons a day. The water is pumped to three elevated storage reservoirs and distributed from these by gravity. The bulk of the water is consumed by domestic users, the government, Kalyani University, and the hospital, but industries are also supplied. The two largest industrial establishments provided most of their water needs from their own tubewells.[1] The supply authority pumps on the average of about one million gallons of water a day and there is very little seasonal variation (Table 17).

The town of Kalyani is a small "model" suburb, 30 miles from Calcutta, just within the northern limits of the Calcutta Metropolitan District. The town was originally laid out in 1953 on the site of a large World War II military base known as Roosevelt Nagar. It was intended that the town should be a new focus for urban development which would relieve the congestion in Calcutta proper. Despite considerable publicity and government interest and a large investment in the basic urban infra-structure, there has been very little development. The development that has occurred has resulted in Kalyani becoming a small middle class suburb with a population largely of civil servants and retired people. There is, in addition, a small industrial estate but very few of the factory employees live in the town because of the relatively high rents charged for the public housing.

At the time of the survey, the end of 1964, there were approximately 900 occupied houses. The majority of these houses were owned by the government and built to two standard designs. In addition, approximately 100 houses were privately owned. There were, in addition, a number of very small houses for low income groups. This last group of houses was not included in the survey as they were not provided with a metered water supply.

---

[1] The two firms, a brewery and a textile machinery manufacturer, are charged a royalty by the Kancharapara Development Agency for their own tubewells. The royalty is at the rate of 12 paise (slightly more than one cent) per 1,000 gallons.

TABLE 17   KALYANI, AVERAGE DAILY SUPPLY OF WATER,
BY SELECTED MONTHS, 1964-1965

Month	Average Daily Supply (Gallons)	Percentage of Average All Months
April	1,130,167	103.5
May	1,078,806	98.8
June	1,082,567	99.1
November	1,033,200	94.6
December	1,083,387	99.2
January	1,142,129	104.6
Annual Average Daily Supply	1,091,869	100.0

SOURCE: Kanchrapara Development Agency.

In the 1961 Census of India, the population of the Kalyani Notified Area was given as 4,616. It was probably very little changed at the time of the survey as there were a large number of unoccupied houses.

The environmental standards adopted in Kalyani are very high. The planned residential density varying between 30-60 persons per acre. All the houses are provided with both a separate bathroom and kitchen and none of the government built houses have less than two rooms. The community has both a continuous water supply, the only town in the Calcutta Metropolitan District so provided, and a waterborne sewerage system.

The high environmental living standards, the relatively high income level, and the continuous supply of water make Kalyani appropriate for studying possible levels of water consumption that might result from improvements in the living environment on a wider scale. Water for domestic consumption is sold to all consumers except the very poor and is priced at 50 paise per 1,000 gallons. [2]

The survey was made on the basis of water consumption data obtained from the meter reading records of the Engineer's Office of the Kancharapara Development Authority.[3]   Continuous

---

[2] About 7 cents (U.S.).

[3] Kalyani is not a municipality but it is administered directly by the West Bengal Government through the Kancharapara Development Authority.

meter records were only available for 574 houses. The sample was reduced by the exclusion of houses which were temporarily unoccupied, houses used as hostels by the Kalyani University and a number of other government colleges, houses used as offices, and houses with defective meters. The consumption data used in the study is for the third quarter of 1964.

A questionnaire (see Appendix A), in English and Bengali, was sent through the mail to all the households for which water consumption data had been obtained. The size of the final sample depended on the number of useable replies received. The analysis has been based on 165 replies, approximately a thirty per cent sample of the households with meter records.

The questionnaire was designed to provide information on three related aspects of water use and consumption:

1. Opinions on direct payment for water and attitudes towards wastage.
2. Information on the water-using habits of and water-using facilities in the household.
3. General information about the household, including the number of people in the family, income, religion, and education which might impinge on the water-use characteristics of the household and the level of water consumption.

The sample households show a large range in per capita consumption, from 1.3 to 165.0 gallons a day. The mean daily per capita consumption is 24.7 gallons but the distribution shows a distinct skew towards the left (Fig. 5). The median consumption is only 20.6 gallons so that the mean is biased by the small number of households with a very high consumption of water (Table 18). The extremes may be due to faulty meters or absence from the house, in the low example, and the presence of guests, in the high. Whatever the reason for the extremes, this would not affect the overall pattern, a pattern maintained through other periods of consumption as well as the period actually used in the analysis. After the questionnaires were completed, meter readings for those households which replied to the questionnaire were obtained for the whole of 1964 in order to observe whether there were any significant seasonal variations in consumption. No significant difference in the daily per capita consumption of water is shown by this data. The lack of seasonal variation is probably due to the absence of extremes

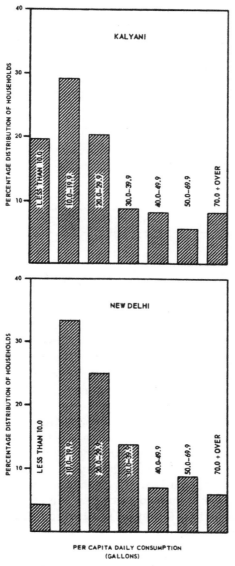

Fig. 5.   Kalyani and New Delhi: Frequency
Distribution of Households by Daily
Per Capita Consumption

in the Calcutta climate and the fact that garden watering is
practised only on a restricted scale.

69

TABLE 18   KALYANI, PER CAPITA DAILY WATER
CONSUMPTION PER DAY (GALLONS)

Per Capita Daily Consumption	Number of Households	Percentage of All Households
less than 10	33	19.5
10 - 19.9	49	29.0
20 - 29.9	34	20.1
30 - 39.9	15	8.9
40 - 49.9	14	8.3
50 - 74.9	10	5.9
75 - 99.9	5	3.0
100 - 124.9	6	3.5
125 and over	3	1.8
TOTAL	169	100.0

Socio-Economic Characteristics

The range of incomes found in Kalyani places the population within the middle income levels for urban areas in India.   Almost three-quarters of the households had incomes of over 200 rupees a month (Table 19).   This can be compared with the average per capita annual income of 327 rupees in West Bengal and the average earnings of West Bengal Government employees, 103 rupees a month. [4]   The middle class nature of Kalyani is further emphasized by the occupations of the heads of households.   The occupational structure reflects the bureaucratic nature of the town.   Half the sample population were directly employed in government, mostly by the West Bengal Government, and a quarter in education and medicine.

Apart from the variations in the levels of income, Kalyani has a homogeneous population.   Over three-quarters of the respondents have had a higher education of one kind or another. The population is mainly Hindu; of the 169 households in the sample, 161 are Hindu.

This homogeneity is also found in the housing.   The public housing has either two or three rooms.   Some of the privately owned houses are larger, but these are very few.   Only half the houses have more than two rooms, but this is a very much

---

[4]West Bengal, State Statistical Bureau, Estimates of State Income and Its Regional Differentials, pp. 10-34.

TABLE 19 KALYANI, INCOME DISTRIBUTION

Income Group (Rupees Per Month)	U.S. Dollars	Number of Households	Percentage of Total Households
less than 200	less than 28.00	45	26.6
201 - 400	28.00 - 53.00	60	35.5
401 - 700	53.00 - 93.00	34	20.1
701 - 1000	93.00 - 134.00	17	10.1
over 1000	over 134.00	13	7.7
TOTAL		169	100.0

higher standard than that of West Bengal as a whole (Table 20). Housing quality is not only reflected in the number of rooms in a house but can be more precisely depicted by the density of occupance, expressed by the number of persons per room. There is a large variation in the density of occupance amongst Kalyani households even given the large proportion of standard housing (Table 21). The number of people per room varies from 0.20 persons to 6.00 persons. The mean density of occupance is 2.02 persons per room. This is a much lower density than that prevailing in central Calcutta or generally in the towns of West Bengal.[5]

The ownership of certain consumer goods can aid the definition of the economic level of the household. Questions were asked on the ownership of three consumer goods—a car, a refrigerator, and a fan. The first two help in the delimitation of the upper income range while the possession of a fan can be used to define the lowest economic level within the sample population. The widespread ownership of fans is a further indication of the high economic level of the population of Kalyani (Table 22).

It can be expected that the relatively high standard of housing would be reflected in the plumbing facilities. Every household has at least two taps and most have in addition a washbasin and shower (Table 23). In comparison, in Calcutta City only 9.2 per cent of households have their own taps.[6] All households

[5]The average number of persons per room in urban areas varies from 2.60 to 4.13 persons in the different districts of West Bengal. In Calcutta, the average number of persons per room is 3.03. India, Census of India, 1961, Vol. XVI: West Bengal and Sikkim, Part IV (1), Report and Main Tables on Housing and Establishments, p. 44.

[6]Sen, Calcutta: A Socio-Economic Survey, pp. 142-143.

TABLE 20   KALYANI AND WEST BENGAL, NUMBER
OF LIVING ROOMS PER HOUSE

| Number of Rooms | Kalyani | | West Bengal |
	Number of Households	Percentage of Households	Percentage of Households*
1 or none	1	0.6	68.5
2	87	51.5	17.2
3	42	24.9	7.0
4	22	13.0	5.6
5 or more	17	10.0	3.7
TOTAL	169	100.0	100.0

*Census of India, 1961, Vol. XVI: West Bengal and Sikkim, Part IV
(1), Report and Main Tables on Housing and Establishments.

TABLE 21   KALYANI, DENSITY OF OCCUPANCE

Persons Per Room	Number of Households	Percentage of All Households
less than 1	21	12.4
1.00 - 1.99	59	34.9
2.00 - 2.99	47	27.8
3.00 - 3.99	31	18.3
4.00 and over	11	6.5

TABLE 22   KALYANI, HOUSEHOLD POSSESSIONS
AND HOUSE OWNERSHIP

Possession	Per Cent of Households Owning
Car	4.1
Refrigerator	7.1
Fan	64.0
House	17.4

possess the minimum of water facilities. A few households
possess more than the minimum. The multiple possession of
taps and other fixtures can be explained by the practice in upper
income households of providing each bedroom with a separate
bathroom.

TABLE 23   KALYANI, POSSESSION OF
WATER-USING FACILITIES

| Facility | Households Possessing | |
	Number	Percentage
Taps 2-3	73	43.2
4-6	80	47.3
7 or more	12	7.1
Sink	65	38.5
Washbasin	158	93.5
Bathtub	9	5.5
Shower	166	98.2
Water heater	10	5.9

Water-Using Habits

The level of water consumption depends not only upon the economic level of the household and the availability of water (expressed through the number of plumbing fixtures), but also upon water-using habits. There are certain domestic activities which can affect the level of water consumption. Questions were asked concerning those activities judged most likely to influence the level of water consumption. These activities were taken to be: (a) bathing, (b) clothes washing, and (c) garden watering.

Elsewhere, the ownership of a flush toilet would also influence variations in the level of water consumption but all households in Kalyani are provided with a flush toilet. It is not relevant, therefore, in this case.

Bathing habits, as could be anticipated with an almost totally Hindu population, do not vary very much between the households. Most of the population bathe once a day in winter and twice a day in the summer (Table 24).

More surprisingly, there is an overwhelming proportion of households which have the clothes washing done by a dhobi, or washerman, outside the house. Only in households with incomes below Rs. 200 a month is there a lesser reliance on the dhobi; households with incomes above Rs. 200 used both a dhobi and washed clothes at home (Table 25). It might be expected that the degree of use of the dhobi would vary. The only information on this aspect is an indication of complete reliance on the dhobi. There were a few households whose entire washing was done by the dhobi but this appears to be less directly related to income

TABLE 24   KALYANI, BATHING HABITS

Number of Baths a Day	Number of Households	Percentage of All Households
Winter		
1	156	92.3
2	12	7.1
3	1	0.6
Summer		
1	26	15.4
2	126	74.6
3	17	10.0

TABLE 25   KALYANI, CLOTHES WASHING

Income Group (Rupees Per Month)	Wash Clothes in House		Dhobi	
	Number of Households	Per Cent	Number of Households	Per Cent
less than 200	33	73.3	24	53.3
201 - 400	49	81.7	49	81.7
401 - 700	29	85.3	30	88.2
701 - 1000	13	76.5	14	82.4
more than 1000	10	77.0	13	100.0
TOTAL	134	79.3	130	77.0

than a function of the size of the household.

Garden watering is again a practice that is widespread in Kalyani, a reflection of the fact that most of the houses stand within a garden. The use of a hose is more restricted and is apparently related to income (Table 26). There is a significantly higher level of income in those households using a hose.

The Kalyani population exhibits a considerable homogeneity both in socio-economic characteristics and patterns of water use. There does appear, however, to be a difference in the water-use habits among that proportion of the population with monthly incomes below 200 rupees and the remainder of the sample. This difference may in part help to explain the wide variations observed in water consumption. The importance of the relationship between water-using habits and income becomes clearer in the analysis that follows.

TABLE 26 KALYANI, GARDEN WATERING

Income Group (Rupees Per Month)	Water Garden		Use Hose	
	Number of Households	Per Cent	Number of Households	Per Cent
less than 200	22	48.9	5	11.1
201 - 400	47	78.3	23	38.4
401 - 700	28	82.4	13	38.3
701 - 1000	17	100.0	11	65.7
more than 1000	13	100.0	10	77.0
TOTAL	127	75.2	62	36.7

Explaining the Pattern of Water Use

The data obtained from the case study were subjected to
multiple correlation analysis. By means of the analysis, the
extent of the interrelationship between the variables used could
be measured together with the strength of the relationship of the
independent variables to the dependent variable, water consumption per capita. The variables used in the analysis included
both the socio-economic characteristics of the households and
the water-using habits. The complete list of the variables used
and the correlation matrix are presented in Appendix B.

The testing of the relationship between the level of water
consumption and the nature of the living environment is rather
disappointing. There is a significant relationship between the
daily average per capita consumption of water and variables ex-
pressing the nature of the living environment (R = 0.56) but the
correlation is weakest in the Kalyani cases. The reason for the
relatively poor performance of the model is most probably the
high degree of homogeneity found in housing conditions, income,
water-use habits, and related aspects of the living environment
among the Kalyani population. A large proportion of the variation in water consumption between households can be ascribed
to leakage and attitudes towards water among the sample population not elicited in this study.

Despite this limitation, the results of the regression analysis do substantiate the hypothesis that water consumption is
related to the living environment. The consumption of water is
closely related to 4 of the 23 variables measured for the Kalyani
population (Table 27). The four variables which explain the

largest proportion of the variations in water consumption represent three aspects of the demand function for water. The significant variables are:

1. The number of taps in a household.
2. Number of baths taken per day in summer.
3. Number of baths taken per day in winter.
4. Household size: number of persons per household.

These four variables represent the effect of income, living conditions, and water-using habits on the level of demand for water. These variables do not exist in isolation but are closely related to other variables used in the analysis; however, they are not themselves significantly related to the level of water consumption.

Number of taps is closely related to all those variables which together form the income characteristic of the household (Table 27). The variables forming the income characteristic are in two groups, the possession of water-using facilities are more general indices of the level of income. In Kalyani, however, the possession of a variety of plumbing fixtures is an index of higher levels of income.

Bathing habits form a separate group of variables and show only an interrelationship with each other ($r = 0.33609$). The number of baths per day in summer and in winter are positively related, although the number of baths taken in summer shows a negative relationship to water consumption and the number of baths in winter a positive relationship. It can be assumed from

TABLE 27   KALYANI, MULTIPLE CORRELATION OF PER CAPITA
WATER CONSUMPTION AND ASPECTS OF THE LIVING
ENVIRONMENT

Variable	Regression Coefficient	t Value	Partial Correlation Coefficient*
Number of taps	0.04362	3.09214	0.23746
Number of baths			
summer	-0.18705	-3.57156	-0.27173
winter	0.23718	2.80851	0.21675
Size of household	-0.07076	-7.18402	-0.49385

R = 0.5623*
F Value = 18.4993*

*Significant at 1 per cent level.

76

the behaviour of these variables that an increasing number of baths in summer is associated with lower income households but this is not clearly shown in the correlation matrix.

The size of household forms a further distinct sector in the water demand function. The size of household is not closely related to income (r = 0.15116) although there is a slight positive relationship between the two variables. Such a relationship would suggest that household size does have some tendency to increase with higher monthly incomes. Size of household is, however, related to the density of occupance variable (r = 0.46749). Substituting density of occupance for size of household, in the multiple correlation expression, reduces the size of the coefficient but shows a similar if less strong relationship. The size of household variable, negatively related to the level of water consumption, does include, therefore, a large density component. Water consumption tends to decrease as the density of occupance rises. ·

Increasing density of occupance of the house probably reduces the accessibility of the occupants to water. Number of taps also to some extent measures the degree of accessibility to water. The analysis shows that with higher levels of income, there is a greater accessibility to water (Table 28)—a relationship which is the corollary of the greater ability of higher income households to use water and therefore to show a higher demand for water.

TABLE 28   KALYANI, SIMPLE CORRELATIONS OF NUMBER
OF TAPS WITH OTHER VARIABLES

Variable	Correlation Coefficient*
Possession of:	
washbasin	0.49193
shower	0.48354
water heater	0.50321
Number of rooms	0.64177
Number of servants	0.46490
Number of servants living in house	0.43594
Income	0.38193
Possession of:	
car	0.37057
refrigerator	0.36700
fan	0.55219

*Significant at 1 per cent level.

77

Fig. 6. Kalyani, a general view
(photo by T. R. Lee).

Fig. 7. A typical three bedroom house
in Kalyani (CMPO photo).

In Kalyani, although a large proportion of the variation in water consumption remains unexplained, there is a significant relationship shown between the level of water consumption and the nature of the living environment. Differences in the living environment are produced not only by income differentials but also by accessibility to water and the water-using habits of the household.

New Delhi

Water Consumption

The water supply of New Delhi, the political capital of the Indian Union, is provided from the Yamuna River. The water supply system of the Delhi area is divided into two separate operations. The supply and distribution of raw water is the responsibility of the Delhi Development Authority. This authority in turn sells the water, at cost, to three distributing authorities, the New Delhi Municipal Committee, the Delhi Cantonment Authorities, and the Delhi Municipal Corporation.[7] The present survey was conducted in New Delhi in the area supplied with water by the New Delhi Municipal Committee.

The average amount of water distributed by the Municipal Committee is 16 million gallons a day, a per capita supply of 61 gallons.[8] The supply is not continuous and is restricted for two periods during the day, 12 a.m. to 3 p.m. and 9 p.m. to 3 a.m.[9] However, many households do enjoy a continuous water supply through the provision of storage tanks on the roofs of the houses.

New Delhi is a modern city laid out in the garden city tradition. In form it is a non-Indian city. The standard of housing and of the overall urban environment is very much higher than that of any other large Indian city. It is, in the residential areas, a larger scale version of the Kalyani type development typical of

---

[7] There are two separate large urban areas which together form the city of Delhi. These are New Delhi, the administrative city established by the British, and the city of Old Delhi, the last capital of the Moghul Emperors.

[8] Interview with A. Malhotra, Municipal Engineer, New Delhi Municipal Committee, November, 1965.

[9] Letter from Raj Narain Garg, Statistician, New Delhi Municipal Committee, December, 1965.

Fig. 8. Class I Housing, Talkatora Road,
New Delhi (Ford Foundation photo).

Fig. 9. Class III Apartment, Laxmibai Nagar,
New Delhi (Ford Foundation photo).

many "new" towns in India. There is, therefore, a high standard of urban amenities and Delhi provides a further example of a situation where high levels of domestic water demand can be anticipated. This case study, however, not only complements the Kalyani one, but extends the range of the survey by providing a greater variety of housing types, income levels, and other socio-economic characteristics.

The population in the areas supplied with water by the New Delhi Municipal Committee was 261,545 in 1961. A sample of 436 households has been used in the study. The source of the sample was the meter record books of the New Delhi Municipal Committee. The period of consumption taken for measurement was September and October, 1965. These were the most recent months for which consumption data were available. It was necessary to have recent data to ensure that the water consumption measured was that of the family currently occupying the house.

A mailed questionnaire was again used for the New Delhi survey. The questionnaire, in English and Hindi, was sent to all the households for which water consumption data had been obtained—1,456 in number. The analysis is based on 436 useable replies. This represents a 30 per cent response to the mailing, a similar rate of response to that obtained in Kalyani, but it forms only 1.8 per cent of the total number of households in New Delhi with metered water supply connections.[10]

The questionnaire used in this case study was basically the same as that used for Kalyani (Appendix A). A number of questions were added to the section concerned with attitudes towards payment for water.

The sample households show a large range in per capita daily water consumption, from 2.3 to 410.0 gallons per day. The mean daily consumption is 29.5 gallons, higher but very close to the Kalyani figure. Reasons why it is higher could be the hotter climate in New Delhi and the discontinuous nature of the water supply. The frequency distribution of per capita consumption is again skewed towards the left (Fig. 5). The median consumption is only 25.2 gallons so that the mean is biased by

---

[10]In March, 1965 there were 23,907 metered water supply connections in the area supplied with water by the New Delhi Municipal Committee (interview with A. Malhotra, Municipal Engineer, New Delhi Municipal Committee, November, 1965).

TABLE 29   NEW DELHI, PER CAPITA
DAILY WATER CONSUMPTION

Per Capita Delhi Water Consumption (Gallons)	Number of Households	Percentage of All Households
less than 10.0	19	4.4
10.0 - 19.9	144	33.0
20.0 - 29.9	108	24.8
30.0 - 39.9	60	13.8
40.0 - 49.9	31	7.1
50.0 - 74.9	42	9.6
75.0 - 99.9	18	4.1
100.0 - 124.0	10	2.3

the small number of households with a very high consumption of water (Table 29).

It was possible to make a more detailed breakdown of consumption patterns by areas within the city. Kalyani could not be differentiated within itself but in New Delhi different parts of the city show considerable variations in socio-economic levels. This is due to the housing policies of the government for the different grades of employees which produces a high degree of uniformity in each neighbourhood. Some 18 different neighbourhoods of the city were included in the survey. It provides an extreme case of the spatial variation in water consumption that would be less clearly shown but present in the normal city (Fig. 10).

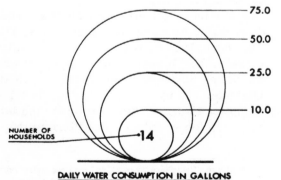

Fig. 10. New Delhi: Mean Per Capita Daily Water Consumption (Gallons) by Subdivisions Surveyed

NUMBER OF HOUSEHOLDS

•14

75.0

50.0

25.0

10.0

DAILY WATER CONSUMPTION IN GALLONS

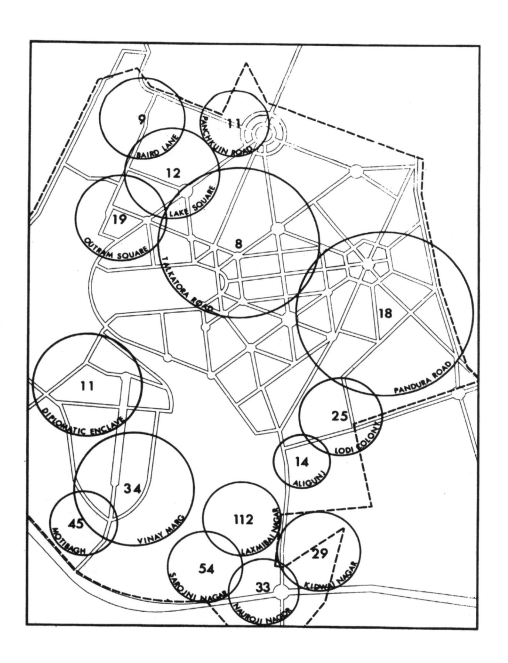

Socio-Economic Characteristics

Any comparison of conditions in New Delhi with the typical Indian urban environment would place New Delhi at a very high level. There is, however, much more variation in the types of housing and in income levels here than in Kalyani. Even the lowest category of housing in New Delhi has metered water connections and there is a relatively large number of very high income households since New Delhi is the centre of government. The majority of the sample population's heads of households are, as in Kalyani, lower- or middle-grade civil servants.

The pattern of income distribution is an illustration of the population structure. Two-thirds of the households have incomes between 200 and 700 rupees a month (Table 30). A larger proportion of the households have incomes of over 1,000 rupees a month than in Kalyani. This could have been anticipated as New Delhi has the highest per capita income of any city in India.

In a population composed entirely of civil servants it can be expected that the level of education would be high; two-thirds of the sample population had some type of higher education. Only five per cent had not attended a secondary school. The entire sample consisted of government employees, the majority in the civil service, and most of the remainder in the armed forces.

Housing in New Delhi is standardized (Table 31). Almost three-quarters of the households live in houses with only two rooms. In addition, all houses have at least a separate kitchen and one bathroom. The standardization of the housing does not produce homogeneity in household size. There is a considerable variation in the number of persons per household (Table 32).

TABLE 30   NEW DELHI, INCOME DISTRIBUTION

Income Group (Rupees Per Month)	U.S. Dollars	Number of Households	Percentage of All Households
less than 100	less-than 14.00	4	0.9
101 - 200	14.00 - 28.00	34	7.8
201 - 400	28.00 - 53.00	172	39.5
401 - 700	53.00 - 93.00	117	26.8
701 - 1000	93.00 - 134.00	27	6.2
over 1000	over 134.00	82	18.8
TOTAL		436	100.0

TABLE 31   NEW DELHI. NUMBER OF
LIVING ROOMS PER HOUSE

Number of Rooms	Number of Households	Percentage of All Households
1	9	2.1
2	321	73.6
3	40	9.2
4	45	10.3
5	14	3.2
6 and over	7	1.6

TABLE 32   NEW DELHI. HOUSEHOLD SIZE

Number of Persons	Number of Households	Percentage of All Households
1	1	0.2
2	12	2.8
3	28	6.4
4	60	13.8
5	90	20.6
6	83	19.0
7	58	13.3
8	53	12.2
9	22	5.0
10 and over	29	6.7

TABLE 33   NEW DELHI, DENSITY OF OCCUPANCE
IN SUBDIVISIONS SAMPLED

Subdivision	Number of Households	Average Household Size	Persons Per Room	Per Capita Daily Water Consumption (Gallons)
Aligunj	14	5.3	2.65	13.8
Baird Lane	9	7.5	3.75	28.1
Diplomatic Enclave	11	4.5	1.07	50.3
Lake Square	12	6.2	1.77	35.2
Lodi Colony	25	6.6	3.00	25.8
Laximibai Nagar	112	6.6	3.30	24.0
Motibagh	45	6.7	3.35	17.7
Naroji Nagar	33	6.6	3.30	19.7
Outram Square	19	6.7	1.91	36.0
Panchkuin Road	11	5.2	4.00	18.9
Pandura Road	18	4.8	1.10	96.2
Kidwai Nagar	29	5.2	2.60	26.2
Sarojni Nagar	54	5.9	2.45	23.1
Vinay Marg	34	4.6	1.28	56.1
Talkatora Road	8	5.1	1.00	91.7
New Delhi All Areas	436	6.0	2.31	29.5

Higher income areas show a larger average size (Table 33).
The density of occupants, expressed as the number of persons
per room, shows an even larger variation from area to area.
The density of occupance ranges from a mean of 4.00 in
Panchkuin Road to less than 1.00 in Pandura Road (Table 33).
The mean density of occupance is 2.31, higher than in Kalyani
but still very low compared to the standards of other urban
areas in India.

The higher income levels found in New Delhi compared to
Kalyani are also shown in the extent of the possession of certain consumer durables. The proportions of households possessing a car, a refrigerator, and a fan are all greater than in
Kalyani (Table 34). The very widespread possession of ceiling
fans is due to the provision of these by the government as a
fringe benefit rather than to the higher income levels.

The standards of housing are repeated in the provision of
plumbing facilities. In this case the standards are not as high
as in Kalyani. Water heaters, the one water-using facility related to income, are more common in New Delhi (Table 35).

TABLE 34   NEW DELHI, HOUSEHOLD POSSESSIONS

Possession	Number of Households Owning	Percentage of All Households
Car	101	23.2
Refrigerator	63	14.5
Fan	423	97.0

TABLE 35   NEW DELHI, POSSESSION OF
WATER-USING FACILITIES

Facility	Households Possessing	
	Number	Percentage
Taps 1	13	3.0
2 - 3	293	67.2
4 - 6	91	20.9
7 and over	39	8.9
Sink	122	28.0
Washbasin	111	25.5
Shower	407	93.4
Water heater	44	10.1
Bathtub	15	3.4

Water-Using Habits

Water consumption is also a function of water-use habits. Questions were asked concerning those activities judged most likely to influence the level of consumption. These activities were again taken to be: (a) bathing, (b) clothes washing, and (c) garden watering.

Most of the sample population, Hindus or not, bathed twice a day in the winter and three times a day in the summer (Table 36). There is no obvious explanation as to why people in New Delhi should bathe more frequently than those in Kalyani. Bathing habits are remarkably constant throughout the population. In contrast, other water habits show a relationship to income.

The majority of households wash some clothes in the home. The proportion of the clothes washing done in the house probably declines as the household income increases. This can be inferred from the increasing use of the dhobi at higher income levels. The proportion of households using a dhobi increases rapidly with incomes of 400 rupees a month and over (Table 37).

Garden watering or irrigation is less common in New Delhi, probably due to the preponderance of apartment buildings over single family housing. The extent of garden watering does increase with higher monthly incomes (Table 38). This is probably partially due to the fact that the upper income families tend to live in houses rather than apartments. There is a similar pattern between income groups in the use of a hose for garden irrigation. It is also likely, however, that gardening is a

TABLE 36   NEW DELHI, BATHING HABITS

Number of Baths a Day	Number of Households*	Percentage of All Households
Winter		
1	69	15.8
2	359	82.5
3	6	1.4
Summer		
1	2	0.5
2	85	19.5
3	348	80.0

*One household reported no bathing in the winter. There was no information on bathing from one household so that the total population is only 435.

TABLE 37   NEW DELHI, CLOTHES WASHING

Income Group (Rupees Per Month)	Wash Clothes in House		Use Dhobi	
	Number of Households	Per Cent	Number of Households	Per Cent
less than 200	37	97.4	6	15.8
201 - 400	159	92.4	80	46.5
401 - 700	110	94.0	82	70.0
701 - 1000	26	96.3	20	74 1
1000 and over*	72	89.9	70	86.5

*Information was not available for one household in this income group.

TABLE 38   NEW DELHI, GARDEN WATERING

Income Group (Rupees Per Month)	Water Garden		Use Hose	
	Number of Households	Per Cent	Number of Households	Per Cent
less than 200	4	10.5	1	2.6
201 - 400	28	16.3	5	2.9
401 - 700	31	26.5	12	10.3
701 - 1000	11	40.8	6	22.2
more than 1000*	51	63.0	44	54.3
TOTAL	125	28.7	68	15.6

*Information was not available for one household in this income group.

response to income per se as well as a function of different living environments. The differentiation found to exist between the various income groups in the degree of the use of the dhobi, garden watering, and the use of a hose has been tested and found significant (less than .001 level).

The administrative nature of New Delhi and its attendant civil service population does not prevent the emergence of considerable variations in the levels of water consumption. The observations made in this study show large differences between households and between parts of the city in the levels of per capita consumption or demand. The explanation of the significance of the different elements which together comprise the de-

mand function for water follows. The analysis will highlight
these factors in the living environment which are the most important in affecting the level of the demand for water.

Explaining the Pattern of Water Use

It was possible to handle the data collected in the Delhi
study in a different way from the analysis performed on the
Kalyani data. The data were aggregated by areas for the city
and the multiple correlation and regression analysis was made
using both the area and household data. Aggregating the data
by area considerably improves the results of the analysis.
There is a very strong relationship shown between the level of
water consumption and higher standards of living environment.
The generalized data, however, only strengthen the relationships already apparent from the use of the household observations.

The multiple correlation and regression analysis of the
New Delhi sample produces better results, even on the household level, than in Kalyani. The reason for this undoubtedly
lies in the greater range of socio-economic characteristics
among the New Delhi population, as well as the greater range
in the level of per capita water consumption. The final model
explains over half the variance in water consumption and there
is a high multiple correlation coefficient (R = 0.7740). The
variables in the final model represent four aspects of the household characteristics which are significant in influencing the per
capita level of consumption. The four groups of characteristics are:
   1. Possession of plumbing facilities.
   2. Water-using habits.
   3. Housing conditions.
   4. The level of income.
There is a considerable degree of interrelationship between the variables. Only one variable, the number of baths
taken per day in the winter, is not significantly related to any
one of the others (Table 39). It is clear from the analysis that
water consumption is positively related to increases in income,
partially through the effects of higher income levels on water
consumption and partially through the influence of the improvement in housing conditions and the adoption of certain water-

TABLE 39   CORRELATION MATRIX OF THE VARIABLES CONSTITUTING
THE MULTIPLE CORRELATION MODEL

	1 Use of Dhobi	2 No. Baths in Winter	3 No. Rooms	4 No. People	5 Income	6 Possession of Refrigerator
1.	1.00000					
2.	0.10966	1.00000				
3.	0.25224	0.08370	1.00000			
4.	-0.18080	-0.01174	-0.23022	1.00000		
5.	0.36078	0.15001	0.62694	-0.23677	1.00000	
6.	0.22320	0.02002	0.70462	-0.32507	0.63121	1.00000

TABLE 40   NEW DELHI, MULTIPLE CORRELATION OF PER CAPITA WATER
CONSUMPTION AND ASPECTS OF THE LIVING ENVIRONMENT

Variable	Regression Coefficient	t Value	Partial Correlation Coefficient
Use of dhobi	0.07713	2.66905	0.18072
Number of baths in winter	0.08209	2.86602	0.19357
Number of rooms	0.06627	4.14468	0.27438
Size of household	0.00623	-5.61489	-0.36055
Income	0.05542	3.77425	0.25148
Possession of refrigerator	0.35471	2.24660	0.15284

$$R = 0.7740*$$
$$F \text{ Value} = 52.5532*$$

*Significant at 1 per cent level.

using habits which are the results of the enjoyment of higher
levels of income (Table 40).

Analyzing the relationships between the level of per capita
water consumption and household characteristics on an aggregate basis improves the performance of the model and strength-
ens the conclusions made from the analysis of the household
data. The analysis of aggregated data produces a very high
correlation coefficient (R = 0.9951). The constituent variables
in the model again represent four aspects of the demand function for water (Table 41). There is, however, a considerable
amount of interrelationship between the variables which would

TABLE 41   NEW DELHI, MULTIPLE CORRELATION OF
PER CAPITA WATER CONSUMPTION AND
ASPECTS OF THE LIVING ENVIRONMENT,
AGGREGATED AREA BASE

Variable	Regression Coefficient	t Value	Fartial Correlation Coefficient
No. taps	0.06207	3.42614	0.75234
Use of dhobi	0.00299	3.83166	0.78737
Size of household	-0.07105	-3.59491	-0.76777
Number of servants	0.14847	5.11105	0.86241
Possession of refrigerator	-0.00261	-3.37495	-0.74740

R = 0.9951*
F Value = 180.5363*

*Significant at 1 per cent level.

underline the importance of income differentials and housing
conditions in influencing the average per capita consumption of
water (see Appendix B, Correlation Matrices).

It is apparent from the results of the analysis of both the
New Delhi and Kalyani case studies that the demand for water
for domestic consumption is strongly related to housing conditions or the quality of the living environment. A large part of
the variations in water consumption remain, however, unexplained by the variables used. The unexplained portion of the
variation is most likely due to differences in individual attitudes
or personalities—differences which are not susceptible to analysis of the type performed in this study.

The possession of multiple plumbing facilities does not
necessarily lead to very high levels of consumption. The living
environment is an important determinate of the demand for water. The demand for water is conditioned by the ability to use
water as well as the accessibility of supply.

91

CHAPTER IV

PATTERNS OF WATER USE AND CONSUMPTION
—BUSTEE AREAS

The second group of case studies is concerned with that section of the urban population dependent on sources of water outside the house. Surveys of water consumption, use, and related socio-economic characteristics were made in six different bustees in the Calcutta area together with a survey of the purposes to which the water from the five available sources was put. Five of the bustees were located in Calcutta and the sixth in Howrah, the city across from Calcutta on the west bank of the River Hooghly.

The number of people interviewed varied from bustee to bustee. The size of the individual samples is a reflection of the actual populations of the bustee areas studied. There was, however, no way to estimate precisely the populations of the different bustees.[1] Consequently it was not possible to ensure a sample of equal proportions from each bustee. There is nothing to suggest, however, that the samples taken are unrepresentative.

The distribution of per capita daily water consumption in Calcutta bustees shows a similar marked skew towards the right as the frequency distributions for Kalyani and New Delhi (Fig. 11). This skew is accompanied, again, by a very large range in per capita consumption (Table 48).

---

[1] Population estimates do exist for all the bustees included within the bustee survey of Calcutta, made by the State Statistical Bureau of the Government of West Bengal, but the information was six years old when the present study was made. An additional factor precluding use of this information was that the population estimates in the Bustee Survey were made for individual bustee land holdings, difficult to identify in the field. See West Bengal, State Statistical Bureau, Report on the Bustee Survey in Calcutta, 1958-59 (Alipore: West Bengal Government Press, 1963), 17 volumes, many unpublished.

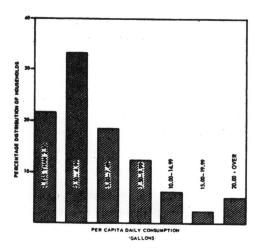

Fig. 11. Calcutta Bustees: Distribution of Households by Per Capita Daily Consumption of Water

This chapter includes a description of the nature of each bustee, in terms of both the physical form of the bustee locality and the dimensions of the water use system, and an analysis of factors affecting the level of the consumption.

Bustee Case Studies

Topsia. —The Topsia bustee is on the eastern edge of the continuous built up area within the boundaries of the city of Calcutta. Compared to the other bustees studied, Topsia is characterized by a low density of development and is bordered on two sides by open land. The huts are clustered around tanks and the tanks occupy approximately one-third of the area of the bustee. Much of the remaining area is very poorly drained and during the monsoon many of the huts are surrounded by water. In contrast to the abundance of surface water, the supply of filtered water obtainable from standpipes is restricted to the paved roads bounding the area on the south and northeast. The only alternative source to the tanks, in the interior of the bustee, is tubewells.

Besides being different physically from the majority of bustees, the Topsia bustee is unusual in having a mixed population, and it is the only sample containing Christians. Income levels are relatively high and a large proportion of the houses are of pukka construction. The general level of education is also high so that on all the social and economic indicators, the population was above the mean for the total bustee sample (Tables 49 and 52).

Not surprisingly, given the relative high standard of the living environment, the mean daily water consumption per capita, 7.11 gallons, is also high. This is despite the paucity of sources other than tanks. The average length of trip for water, therefore, is long. The actual distances are:

1. Standpipe - 65 yards.
2. Pump - 92 yards.
3. Tank - 82 yards.

The length of trip is longest for the pump but this does not appear to inhibit use of the pump, as an equal number of respondents made use of the pump and standpipe. There is a restraint, the limited hours of supply, on the availability of water from the standpipe. The average length of trip to the tank is rather surprisingly long given the number of tanks in this bustee. Many of the tanks are, however, in the interior of the bustee, while much of the housing is around the edge. It could also be merely a reflection of under-reporting of use by those households nearest to the tanks.

The frequency of use of the different sources for different purposes shows the much greater use of the pump and standpipe than of any other source. The tank is used for approximately one-tenth of the water activities—a high proportion

TABLE 42   USE OF WATER ACCORDING TO ORIGIN, TOPSIA

| Purpose | Origin | | | |
	Standpipe	Pump	Tank	Unfiltered Hydrant
	Number of Respondent Households			
Drinking	17	19	–	–
Cooking	17	18	1	–
Washing Clothes	16	12	8	–
Washing Dishes	16	15	4	1
Bathing	18	12	6	–
Percentage of all Use by Households	46.6	42.2		0.6

compared to other bustees and related to the general availability of tank water. The tank is used, however, by only one household for consumption purposes (cooking), otherwise use is restricted to washing (Table 42).

The large number of tanks in the Topsia bustee does affect the source-use pattern but there is still a heavy reliance on the better quality water available from the standpipe and pump. The relationship between quality and use will be discussed in more detail later, but from the pattern of uses observed in this bustee, it appears that there are quality judgments which affect the use made of the different water sources.

Goabagan. —The Goabagan bustee is located in the north-central part of Calcutta, that part of the city originally called the "native town. " It is a densely developed area with a variety of small workshops intermingling with a residential use of the bustee. The main street frontage of the bustee is occupied by motor vehicle repair and part shops and at the northern end there is a large kattal or cattle shed. Many of the huts are of two stories with small workshops on the ground floor. The bustee is laid out in a grid pattern with access provided by paved footpaths.

Goabagan is well supplied with both pumps and standpipes along the footpaths and bounding roads. The latter are also the site of a number of unfiltered water hydrants. Some of the huts had individual house connections but water was only available for a very limited part of the day. In contrast, the public taps had an almost continuous supply, although at a low pressure and with interruptions in the flow for short periods. There were no tanks in the immediate vicinity of the bustee although there was one large tank 150 yards to the south. This tank had been converted into a swimming pool which would restrict its use for other purposes, but people were observed washing in the tank during the survey.

All the respondents in this bustee were Hindu. The income distribution of the households was similar to the pattern for all bustees. The size of the households was the highest in any of the bustees surveyed, more than seven persons, possibly an indication of joint messing arrangements.[2]

---

[2]A house or room occupied jointly by a number of single men.

The mean daily consumption of water per capita was the highest, 7.53 gallons, of any bustee in the survey. One-third of the households, however, consumed less than two gallons per day and one-third over eight. The range in per capita consumption was less than in Topsia but still very great, from less than one gallon to more than twenty-five. The source complex in Goabagan consists of standpipes, tubewells, and the unfiltered hydrants. The mean distances travelled to collect water from the different sources were:
1. Standpipe - 18 yards.
2. Pump - 19 yards.

Only two respondents made use of the unfiltered hydrant so that the distance travelled cannot be justifiably used to suggest any trend, but as elsewhere, when use was made of the unfiltered hydrant, the hydrant was within five yards of the house.

The length of the water trip was similar for both the standpipe and the pump. The short length of trip emphasizes the high density of occurrence of these two water sources in the bustee. The use distribution between the sources does show the influence of the high rate of provision of standpipes. There is a marked concentration of use at the standpipe, particularly for consumption uses, drinking and cooking (Table 43). The use of the other sources for non-consumption uses, but uses requiring large amounts of water, represents an adjustment to the low pressure and the more difficult access to the filtered water.

TABLE 43   USE OF WATER ACCORDING TO ORIGIN, GOABAGAN

Purpose	Origin			
	Standpipe	Pump	Tank	Unfiltered Hydrant
	Number of Respondent Households			
Drinking	18	3	-	-
Cooking	21	-	-	-
Washing Clothes	11	7	2	1
Washing Dishes	9	7	2	3
Bathing	10	9	2	1
Percentage of all Use by Households	65.0	24.6	5.7	4.7

There appears here again to be an awareness of the quality differences between the types of available water. The high proportionate use made of the standpipe can be traced also to the availability of filtered water, both the number of standpipes and the continuous supply.

Tollygunge. —The Tollygunge bustee covers a large area at the junction of two of the major roads in south Calcutta. It is situated immediately to the north of the Tollygunge Racecourse, part of one of the large clubs established by the British, and to the west is bounded by Tolly's Nullah, a small stream draining into the Hooghly. The street frontage of the bustee is largely occupied by shops of both kutcha and pukka construction. Entry to the bustee is mainly by narrow lanes, although there is one broader road lined with shops.

The bustee can be subdivided into three smaller units. The three areas are:

1. Largely pukka housing with paved paths and good drainage adjacent to the Tollygunge Circular Road—Russa Road Junction.

2. Kutcha housing along the bank of Tolly's Nullah and a subsidiary drainage channel dividing the bustee from the racecourse. Both drainage and housing are very poor.

3. A second area of kutcha housing, in the southeast corner of the bustee, divided from the first by a number of middle class houses behind walls. The huts are built around small tanks or other open space. Drainage is poor.

All the water sources are available in this bustee, although not equally to the different sections. The filtered water is not continuous in supply and the tubewell pumps suffer severely from silting. Tolly's Nullah and the other drainage channel are both heavily polluted with sewage. The banks of the streams are used for kattals which adds to the pollution. The Nullah is used for navigation by country boats although there are no wharves in the bustee.

The population of the bustee is mainly Hindu with a small minority of Moslems. The average size of the household is only five persons, the smallest in any of the bustees. The Hindu population has generally a higher level of education than the Moslems, although there is no significant difference in income levels.

There is a marked difference in the average per capita consumption of water between the households in the first two areas
and those in the third. The average per capita consumption in
the former was 5.92 gallons per day and in the latter, 7.93
gallons. The difference between the two areas lies in the availability of water sources; sources were less abundant in the
third area. The explanation of the higher consumption would be
in terms of lesser use of the water at source and greater use
at home. The mean per capita water consumption for the whole
bustee is 6.59 gallons per day. Variations in per capita consumption may also be related to differences in household size;
in area three, the average household size is smaller, 3.9 persons, than areas one and two, 5.75 persons.

Most of the respondents used only the standpipe and the
pump as sources of water. The average length of trip to the
two sources was:
1. Standpipe - 29 yards.
2. Pump - 122 yards.

The length of the trip to the pump can be explained by the
less frequent occurrence of pumps, particularly as many of the
existing pumps were not working. Water trip distances were
not obtained for the other sources except for one respondent
using the Nullah. There is almost complete reliance on the
standpipe for every use except drinking (Table 44). This can
be related to the mechanical deficiencies of the pumps in
Tollygunge. The local population was very insistent on this
point during the survey. A more difficult result to explain is

TABLE 44   USE OF WATER ACCORDING
TO ORIGIN, TOLLYGUNGE

Purpose	Origin		
	Standpipe	Pump	Ganges Water
	Number of Respondent Households		
Drinking	27	15	-
Cooking	37	5	-
Washing Clothes	36	6	-
Washing Dishes	35	6	1
Bathing	35	6	1

the use of the pump as a source of drinking water but this may be due to a taste preference for the ground water. The neglect of the streams as a source may be due to the poor quality of the water together with the difficulty of access in most parts of the bustee. Each use tends to demand particular requirements of the water source but this is not the only factor; accessibility is also important.

Beniapukur. —Beniapukur is part of a vast complex of bus-tee development along the southeastern fringe of the centre of Calcutta. It is at the western edge of the complex adjacent to a major road junction known as Park Circus. The bustee is densely developed with the exception of the northern edge where there is open land. There is only one paved lane through the bustee; the other lanes are merely dirt tracks. There is no clear pattern to the bustee but it is a maze of huts separated by narrow alleys, many with dead ends. The western edge of the bustee is fringed with small shops and workshops. Despite the high density of development within the bustee, the huts are predominantly of pukka construction.

There is a lack of sources of water supply in this bustee. There are no tanks or surface streams close by and in the southern half there are few sources in the interior. Standpipes, pumps, many broken and unfiltered hydrants are located along the streets bounding the bustee and the one paved path through it.

Beniapukur has almost an entirely Moslem population; only three of the fifty households interviewed were Hindu. The density of occupance is high as the average number of rooms per household is low, but the average size of households above the mean for all bustees. Income levels are lower than in the Hindu majority bustees and the proportion of the population without education is higher (Tables 49 and 52).

The mean daily per capita consumption of water is only 3.88 gallons, slightly more than half that in the bustees previously discussed. The low consumption could be connected with different water-using habits among Moslems. For example, Moslems tend to bathe less often and less copiously than Hindus. The distance to the water sources, the average trip length, is high but not sufficiently longer than elsewhere to account for any difference in consumption. Water trip measurements were only obtained for the standpipe and pump. The

TABLE 45   USE OF WATER ACCORDING
TO ORIGIN, BENIAPUKUR

Purpose	Origin		
	Standpipe	Pump	Tank
	Number of Respondent Households		
Drinking	50	-	-
Cooking	50	-	-
Washing Clothes	41	9	-
Washing Dishes	40	10	-
Bathing	37	12	1
Percentage of all Use by Households	87.4	14.2	0.4

distances were as follows:
1.   Standpipe - 64 yards.
2.   Pump - 31 yards.

The shorter trip length to the pump is not in this case due
to the number of pumps but the particular location of the pumps
in the bustee. There were no pumps accessible from the southern part of the bustee.

Despite the availability of the unfiltered water, none of the
respondents reported making use of it (Table 45). The use pattern shows a heavy concentration of use on the standpipe, particularly for drinking and cooking. The use of the pump was
restricted to those purposes requiring larger amounts of water.
The necessity to rely on the standpipe may in itself act as a
restraint upon consumption due to the discontinuity in the supply
from this source.

Saheb Bagan. —Saheb Bagan also lies within the ring of
bustees around the centre of the city. It is situated on the west
bank of the Circular Canal and is part of a large area of bustee,
but is separated from the remainder by major streets. The
bustee, itself, is divided into a number of smaller units by
paved roads accessible to motor traffic. Except in the northeast corner, most of the huts are laid out in a grid pattern.
The road frontages, as in most bustees, are lined with shops
and there is a market in the southwest corner. There are a
large number of multi-storied brick buildings in the bustee as
well as the huts.

All water sources, except tanks, are available to the bustee population. The canal is only directly accessible from the bustee at one point. The remainder of the bustee is cut off from the canal by factories and a police station. The canal bank is used for keeping cattle and similar activities. Water for the cattle is taken from the canal despite the fact that the canal is stagnant and very dirty. Among the other water sources, standpipes are most numerous along the larger streets; in the interior of the bustee, the landlords and not the municipal authorities are responsible for water supply. In addition to the usual water sources, there are a number of public latrines and a public wash house.

Saheb Bagan is largely inhabited by Moslems, although there is a small Hindu population. Incomes in the bustee are relatively low, compared to the other bustees surveyed, and housing conditions poor. The density of occupance was very similar to that found in Beniapukur. The level of education of the respondents was even lower than in Beniapukur, the other predominately Moslem bustee.

The average daily per capita water consumption was 4.79 gallons, a figure somewhat above that for Beniapukur. It is perhaps related to the greater accessibility of water sources in Saheb Bagan. The length of the water trip in Saheb Bagan was: ·

1. Standpipe - 28 yards.
2. Pump - 19 yards.

Three respondents made use of unfiltered hydrants and two of the canal. The trip length to the canal was the greatest, 42 yards. In both cases, the canal water was used by respondents keeping cattle.

Use of the standpipe is dominant, particularly for drinking and cooking. Those uses requiring larger amounts are again the purposes for which other sources are used. One peculiar feature of the source-use distribution is the small amount of use of the pump water for cooking (Table 46). This can be related to the feeling of some respondents that the ground water is hard and unsuitable for cooking rice. The unfiltered hydrant was more widely used in Saheb Bagan than in any other bustee, a reflection of the availability of this water source inside the bustee as well as around the edge.

101

TABLE 46   USE OF WATER ACCORDING TO ORIGIN, SAHEB BAGAN

Purpose		Origin		
	Standpipe	Pump	Unfiltered Hydrant	Ganges Water
		Number of Respondent Households		
Drinking	55	10	-	-
Cooking	62	3	-	-
Washing Clothes	39	20	6	-
Washing Dishes	41	17	6	1
Bathing	41	19	5	-
Percentage of all Use by Households	73.3	21.2	5.2	0.3

Pilkhana. —The Pilkhana bustee is the only one of the bustees surveyed located outside the municipal boundaries of Calcutta. It is a very large bustee in Howrah, to the west of the Grand Trunk Road, the main highway from Calcutta to New Delhi. The bustee covers an area of approximately sixty acres between the highway and the yards of the Eastern Railway to the west. The frontage of the bustee on the highway is lined with shops and there are other shopping centres along the main paved lanes within the bustee. There are many workshops within the bustee, particularly for the manufacture of pottery, steel trunks, and chains. In total, the structure of Pilkhana is more complex than that of any of the other bustees surveyed.

Water supply and drainage is poor. There are public standpipes but inside the bustees the water mains are choked and there is consequently no supply. The population rely on pumps for their water supply, and there is one tank.

Pilkana is unusual in that it has a mixed Moslem and Hindu population. There is slightly less overcrowding here than in the predominately Moslem bustees; the average size of households is smaller and the number of rooms greater. The level of education in the bustee is between that found in the Hindu and Moslem majority areas. The level of income is similar to that for all bustees.

The per capita mean daily consumption of water was 5.07 gallons. The length of the water trips were:

TABLE 47   USE OF WATER ACCORDING
TO ORIGIN, PILKHANA

| | Origin | | |
Purpose	Standpipe	Pump	Tank
	Number of Respondent Households		
Drinking	32	30	-
Cooking	32	30	-
Washing Clothes	22	38	2
Washing Dishes	23	38	1
Bathing	24	36	2
Percentage of all Use by Households	42.9	55.5	1.6

1. Standpipe - 42 yards.
2. Pump - 61 yards.

The longer trip to the pump indicates the low provision of pumps, even in those parts of the bustee dependent on this source of water. A few respondents did use the tank and the unfiltered hydrants; in all cases these households were very close to the source.

There is less total reliance on the standpipe in Pilkhana, although it remains the most common source for drinking and cooking water (Table 47). The pump is the dominant source used for all other purposes. The use of the tank is restricted by its eccentric location within the bustee. Three respondents kept cattle and used the tank and the unfiltered hydrant as a source of water for the cattle. The importance of the pump in the use complex is directly related to the inadequacies of the standpipe and the size of the bustee which precludes the use of the more distant standpipes in the unsupplied part of the bustee. In Howrah, as in Calcutta, the filtered water supply is not provided continuously and this also affects the degree to which the standpipes can be relied upon. It is likely that quality differences in the water are of less significance here with the absence of alternative sources of supply.

103

Explaining the Pattern of Water Use

The differentiation within the bustee population is greater than that found in the metered areas. There is more variation in the elements which comprise the water-use system. Detailed consideration of the characteristics outlined here will be left for a later discussion. One element within the system will be discussed more thoroughly—the significance of differences in the nature of the actual sources themselves. The discussion is in two parts: (1) the purposes for which the different sources are used, and (2) opinions about the quality of the different types of water among the user population.

Uses Made of the Different Sources

An important consideration of domestic water consumption and use by the population dependent upon public water facilities is the purpose for which the different sources are used. This aspect of water use is particularly significant for the planning of the introduction of new public water sources as a public health measure.

Some consideration of this question has been given by the study of water use in bustee households. In addition, surveys were made of the use of water from the various sources and also of those water-using activities performed at each source. These observations show considerable differences in the use made of the sources, differences common to the three different surveys made.

TABLE 48   CALCUTTA BUSTEES, PER CAPITA
DAILY WATER CONSUMPTION

Bustee	Average Daily Water Consumption (Gallons)	Size of Sample
Topsia	7.11	36
Goabagan	7.53	21
Tollygunge	6.59	42
Beniapukur	3.88	50
Saheb Bagan	4.79	67
Pilkhana	5.07	62
All Bustees (weighted mean)	5.41	279

The household survey may underestimate the amount of use of the "unsafe" sources, although at least one source of an unsafe kind was available in each bustee surveyed. Standpipes and pumps were generally the most accessible sources and the survey revealed an overwhelming use of water from either the standpipe or the pump for all purposes (Table 55).

Every respondent claimed to use the standpipe or pump for drinking water. There is a greater concentration of use of the standpipe for drinking and cooking than for other purposes. The domination of the standpipe for cooking water would seem to be due to the hardness of the water from the pump.[3] For the

TABLE 49 CALCUTTA BUSTEES, INCOME DISTRIBUTION

Bustee	Monthly Income				
	Less than Rupees 50	Rupees 51-100	Rupees 101-150	Rupees 151-200	Over Rupees 200
Topsia	-	12	18	4	2
Goabagan	2	8	8	3	-
Tollygunge	3	20	15	1	3
Beniapukur	6	26	11	5	1
Saheb Bagan	4	40	13	4	2
Pilkhana	1	29	24	7	1
All Bustees	16	135	89.	24	9
Percentage	5.9	49.5	32.6	8.7	3.3

[3] The total hardness of the groundwater is much greater than that of the water of the Hooghly River.

Hooghly-Total Hardness, $CaCO_3$ (ppm) 60-90

Groundwater-Total Hardness, $CaCO_3$ (ppm) 410

SOURCE: CMPO, "Survey of Water Supply Resources of Greater Calcutta," Status Report of the UN Special Fund, World Health Organization, Project India—170, March, 1965. The softness of water appears to be an important quality of water used for cooking from the response to questions asked about water quality. Ninety out of 225 persons who replied to this question stressed softness as a positive quality of water used for cooking. Sixty-two out of the 90 gave softness as an attribute of the filtered water.

TABLE 50 CALCUTTA BUSTEES. HOUSEHOLD SIZE

Bustee	1-2 Persons	3-5 Persons	6-9 Persons	10 and More Persons
Topsia	4	16	10	6
Goabagan	1	9	6	5
Tollygunge	5	26	9	2
Beniapukur	3	10	32	6
Saheb Bagan	2	24	25	15
Pilkhana	2	21	31	8
All Bustees	17	106	113	42
Percentage	6.1	38.1	40.7	15.1

TABLE 51 CALCUTTA BUSTEES, BATHING HABITS

Bustee	Number of Baths Per Day					
	Summer			Winter		
	1	2	3 or More	1	2	3 or More
Topsia	5	23	8	28	7	1
Goabagan	3	14	4	14	6	1
Tollygunge	1	37	4	39	3	-
Beniapukur	18	33	-	50	1	-
Saheb Bagan	6	60	-	65	1	-
Pilkhana	24	38	-	60	2	-
All Bustees	57	205	16	256	20	2
Percentage	20.5	73.7	5.8	92.1	7.2	0.7

TABLE 52 CALCUTTA BUSTEES, LEVEL OF EDUCATION

Bustee	None	Primary	Secondary	College
Topsia	7	11	13	5
Goabagan	3	9	6	3
Tollygunge	10	19	11	2
Beniapukur	28	14	7	2
Saheb Bagan	49	14	3	-
Pilkhana	21	30	9	2
All Bustees	118	97	49	14
Percentage	42.5	34.9	17.6	5.0

106

TABLE 53   CALCUTTA BUSTEES, RELIGIOUS GROUPS

Bustee	Hindu	Moslem	Christian	Other
Topsia	17	12	7	-
Goabagan	21	-	-	-
Tollygunge	39	3	-	-
Beniapukur	3	47	-	1
Saheb Bagan	11	55	-	-
Pilkhana	27	33	-	1
All Bustees	119	150	7	2
Percentage	42.8	54.0	2.5	0.8

other purposes identified, there was a lesser use of the stand-pipe compared to the pump and some use of the other sources.

The characteristics of water use shown in the household survey have been substantiated by surveys conducted at the various sources. Two surveys were made, one based on short interviews with the users at the sources and the second on the observation of the use made of the sources.

The user survey shows a similar variation in the use made of water from the standpipe and pump compared to other sources (Table 56). The tank, unfiltered hydrant, and the river are mainly used for bathing and washing clothes. In contrast, the standpipe and the pump are used for all purposes, although they are less popular for non-consumption purposes requiring large amounts of water. The pump water again appears to be proportionately less used for cooking compared to the filtered water from the standpipe. The differences in the frequency of use of the different sources for different purposes was tested by chi square and found to be statistically significant at the .001 level. This result raises the question of why there should be a difference between the purposes to which the water from the various sources is put.

Observations of the use made of the water at the different sources were made to examine the significance of convenience in use as a factor influencing the water-use activities performed at the various sources. The advantage of the tank, unfiltered hydrant, and the river is that the water is available easily and in unlimited quantity. The water supplied through the standpipe or pump is more difficult to use when large quantities are required.

TABLE 54 NUMBER OF TRIPS TO COLLECT WATER AT DIFFERENT DISTANCES

Bustee	Less than 10		10-19		20-29		30-39		40-99		100 and Over	
	Standpipe	Pump	Standpipe	Pump	Standpipe	Pump	Standpipe	Pump	Standpipe	Pump	Standpipe	Pump
Topsia	2	2	2	–	2	3	6	3	3	4	4	7
Goabagan	7	3	7	2	3	1	–	2	4	1	–	–
Tollygunge	4	1	9	2	12	2	1	–	8	1	2	4
Beniapukur	–	–	9	2	6	2	6	–	20	3	9	–
Saheb Bagan	2	2	24	7	14	7	4	–	6	1	3	–
Pilkhana	2	–	4	3	6	6	6	6	8	12	2	7
All Bustees	17	8	55	16	43	21	23	11	49	22	20	18
Percentage*	8.2	8.3	26.6	16.7	20.8	21.9	11.1	11.5	23.7	22.9	9.7	18.8

*Percentage of the total number of trips to the Standpipe and the Pump separately.

108

TABLE 55   USE OF WATER ACCORDING
TO ORIGIN, BUSTEE SURVEY

Purpose	Origin				
	Standpipe	Pump	Tank	Unfiltered Hydrant	Ganges Water
	Number of Respondent Households				
Drinking	201	77	-	-	-
Cooking	221	56	1	-	-
Washing Clothes	167	92	12	7	-
Washing Dishes	166	93	7	10	2
Bathing	167	93	11	6	1
TOTAL Use*	222	112	13	10	2

*Total Use is the number of households who used the source for any purpose.

TABLE 56   USE OF WATER ACCORDING TO
ORIGIN, SOURCE SURVEY

Purpose	Origin				
	Standpipe	Pump	Tank	Unfiltered Hydrant	Hooghly Water
	Number of Users				
Drinking	84	103	-	1	3
Cooking	85	83	2	1	3
Washing Clothes	52	50	49	11	16
Washing Dishes	48	47	16	9	8
Bathing	56	58	58	12	49
TOTAL Number of Users	98	118	59	16	49

The most difficult source to use in situ is the pump and it is mainly used to collect water for use in the home (Table 57). The standpipe is also used to collect water but much water is used at the standpipe itself. In contrast, very little water is taken away from the other sources.

The differences, in the uses to which the water at the different sources is put, is again very marked. The tank and the unfiltered hydrant are not used for consumption purposes and are almost entirely used at the source. The pump and

109

TABLE 57   THE USE MADE OF WATER
AT SELECTED ORIGINS

Origin	Fetching Water	Washing Clothes	Bathing	Washing Dishes	Washing
	Number of Users				
Standpipe	73	33	57	19	111
Pump	224	15	32	14	54
Tank	4	52	51	4	47
Unfiltered hydrant	1	1	2	1	22

standpipe water, particularly the former, is taken away from the source for use.   The differences in the distribution of uses was again statistically significant (X_2 [chi square] test, .001 level) and supports the contention of the importance of attributes of the source in the uses to which the water is put.

A similar pattern of water activities was shown by the results of the source user survey.   The pump and standpipe were more heavily used than the other sources—the tank, unfiltered hydrant, and the Hooghly.   The latter tended to be used for one or more specific purposes (Table 56).   The distribution was tested by means of chi square and found to be significant at the .001 level (for the test the data were aggregated).

The results indicate that the population dependent upon public water sources discriminates between the different sources. This discrimination affects the purposes to which any particular water type is put.   One of these factors is the mode of occurrence, especially important when large quantities are needed. This, however, of itself cannot explain the use pattern.   The recognition of quality differences would also seem to play an important role in the observed use patterns.

Judgment or Perception of Water Quality
The opinions of judgments of water quality formed part of the bustee household survey.   An open-ended question was asked during the interview on the quality of the water obtained from each source.   The replies to this question have been classified into three groups: (a) those giving a good opinion, (b) those con-

110

TABLE 58 OPINIONS OF WATER FROM DIFFERENT ORIGINS

Source	Good		Some Criticism		Bad	
	Users	Non-Users	Users	Non-Users	Users	Non-Users
Standpipe	206	32	15	2	-	-
Pump	87	167	5	8	2	2
Tank	5	39	1	4	4	18
Unfiltered hydrant	1	2	5	56	3	69
River or canal	-	1	-	50	2	82

taining some criticism but not sufficiently critical to preclude use, and (c) those condemning the source.[4]

As could be anticipated from the use pattern, there was very little criticism of the water obtained from the standpipes or pumps and general condemnation of the water taken from the unfiltered hydrant and the river or canals (Table 58). The tank water was regarded more ambivalently and was the only one of the "unsafe" sources to be given a majority of good opinions. It can be hypothesized that this is partially due to the traditional role of the tank in Bengal, and other parts of India, as a source of water supply and a feature of the living environment.[5]

The distribution of answers also suggests the importance of the physical appearance of the water in the making or perception of the judgment of quality. The physical quality of the tank water tends to be superior to that of the water from either the unfiltered hydrant, the river, or the canals. Water from these last sources, "Ganges Water, " has a high silt content and is often salt, especially in the hot season.[6]

There is a significant statistical difference between the opinions of users and non-users (Table 58). Users tend to have a higher opinion of the source than non-users (chi square .001). This could be due to the greater use made of the standpipe and

---

[4]The questions were not answered in all cases. It was difficult to obtain a valid opinion when the respondent was not familiar with all the water sources.

[5]See Jacqueline Tyrwhitt, ed., Patrick Geddes in India for an account of the place of the tank in the Indian urban scene.

[6]In June, 1966, the salt content of the Hooghly River water reached 3,080 parts per million (sodium chloride), the highest on record (The Statesman [Calcutta], June 9, 1966).

pump giving a bias to the quality opinions but confirming the importance of quality in the source decision.

These observations suggest a general awareness of the superior quality of the water obtained from the standpipe or pump. This water is particularly preferred for cooking and drinking where there is most danger of illness from the use of contaminated water. It can be assumed that quality differences in the water of the various sources do have an influence on the water-use pattern adopted by the population dependent upon public sources of supply.

The description of the nature of water consumption and use suggests some of the important elements in the living environment that impinge on the water demand situation. The nature of the relationship between elements in the living environment and the level of the demand for water needs a more thorough analysis.

The Level of Water Consumption

The variables for which data were obtained by means of the interviews were subjected to a multiple correlation and regression analysis. The results of the analysis show a more complex relationship between water consumption, water-using habits, and the living environment in the bustees compared to areas with individual house connections.

Variations in the level of water consumption are related to four variables. These variables are:
1. The number of trips made to fetch water from the standpipe.
2. The number of trips made to fetch water from the pump.
3. Use of the dhobi.
4. Household size.

The first two variables represent the extent of the use made of either the pump or the standpipe. As might be expected, there is a high positive correlation between the level of consumption and the number of trips made to collect water (Table 59). The trip variables do not, however, really explain why the level of consumption varies.

These variables were substituted for water consumption as the dependent variable in two further multiple correlation anal-

112

Fig. 12. Interior of Saheb Bagan Bustee with
pukka huts (CMPO photo).

Fig. 13. Standpipe and pump, South
Calcutta (photo by T. R. Lee).

Fig. 14.   Tank with latrine, Topsia
(photo by T. R. Lee).

Fig. 15.   Bathing at an unfiltered water
hydrant (photo by T. R. Lee).

114

Fig. 16. Queuing for water
(CMPO photo).

Fig. 17. Multiple use ornamental tank,
Wellesley Street (photo by
T. R. Lee).

TABLE 59   CALCUTTA BUSTEES, MULTIPLE CORRELATION OF PER
CAPITA WATER CONSUMPTION AND SELECTED VARIABLES

Variable	Regression Coefficient	t Value	Partial Correlation Coefficient
No. trips:			
Standpipe	0.03087	11.76207	0.58064
Pump	0.03379	15.37188	0.68182
Use of dhobi	0.05113	2.51053	0.15049
Household size	-0.05515	-14.36247	-0.65673

R = 0.7891*
F Value = 89.7943*

*Significant at 1 per cent level.

yses.   The decision to use these variables was based on the
reduction in the multiple correlation coefficient when they were
excluded (the highest multiple correlation coefficient obtained
was R = 0.5722).

The use of the dhobi variable appears in the model partially
as an expression of the accessibility of water.   There is a positive relationship to income (r = 0.15160).   All households in the
highest income group make use of the dhobi, while less than a
quarter do in the lowest income group.   Use of the dhobi is also
positively related to the number of times that the household was
required to queue in order to obtain water (r = 0.57777).

The size of household in the bustees, as in the metered
areas, is a very significant factor in influencing the level of
water consumption.   The larger household consumes less water.
In the bustee it is likely that more of the consumption occurs at
the source rather than in the house as the size of the household
increases.

The outstanding feature of the correlation analysis is the
omission of the distance variable from the model.   The simple
correlation between water consumption and distance to both the
standpipe and the pump, all subjected to a logarithmic trans-
formation, are both significant at the 5 per cent level, standpipe r = 0.1382, pump r = 0.28039, but neither are significant
constituents of the multiple correlation.   The positive correlation of distance from the pump with water consumption can be
explained by the tendency for pump users to be a long distance

TABLE 60 CALCUTTA BUSTEES, MULTIPLE CORRELATION
OF TRIPS TO PUMP AND SELECTED VARIABLES

Variable	Regression Coefficient	t Value	Partial Correlation Coefficient
Bathing at home	0.24555	2.00809	0.12109
Queue	-1.15420	-2.45877	-0.14772
Buying water	3.43775	3.34368	0.19905
Income	0.76106	2.68439	0.16904
Distance to standpipe	-1.34134	-3.19683	-0.19063
Pump	4.28069	11.10839	0.55935

R = 0.7056*
F Value = 44.7729*

*Significant at 1 per cent level.

TABLE 61 CALCUTTA BUSTEES, MULTIPLE CORRELATION OF
TRIPS TO STANDPIPE AND SELECTED VARIABLES

Variable	Regression Coefficient	t Value	Partial Correlation Coefficient
Size of household	0.30244	3.67111	0.21690
Ability to read Bengali	2.33163	3.77830	0.22292
Distance to standpipe	1.44466	3.25595	0.19334
Pump	-1.44578	-3.49587	-0.20700

R = 0.4628*
F Value = 18.6008*

*Significant at 1 per cent level.

from both sources and not the pump alone. There is a distinct
preference for the standpipe among all users. Use of the pump
is largely dictated by lack of accessibility to a standpipe. The
number of trips to collect water increases with distance both
for the pump and the standpipe (Tables 60 and 61).

The number of trips to the pump is also related to bathing
habits. The number of trips increases when the bathing is done

117

at the house. There is a negative relationship shown between queueing and the number of trips, emphasizing the influence of accessibility to the source on the level of consumption. Income appears to be significant in influencing the number of trips to the pump but not to the standpipe. The differences in the two models are due to differences in accessibility to the sources in the different bustees. In the predominantly Moslem bustees there were less standpipes. The greater number of standpipes in Hindu areas leads to the use of the pump being restricted to households with a high demand or households most distant from the standpipes.

The patterns of water use and consumption in the bustees is very much influenced by the problems of collecting water from a source outside the house. The level of consumption is affected by accessibility to a source. The nature of the living environment does also, however, influence levels of consumption and the nature of water use. Similar influences can be discerned operating among the bustee households as were found to be important in the analysis of water consumption in households with individual connections. There are important differences introduced by the problem of accessibility, particularly to the filtered water standpipes, but there are also important similarities. Large households again show lower consumptions than small. Living conditions are an important part of the demand function for water in the bustees as well as in areas of good housing.

CHAPTER V

CONCLUSIONS AND POLICY IMPLICATIONS

A public water supply is only one among the social overhead
facilities necessary to support a developing economy. Policy
towards the provision of water supplies must be based on an
understanding of the place of a water supply system in the wider
context of the role of social overhead investment in the development process. Current policy, however, tends to view water
supply in isolation. Similarly, little consideration is given to
the demand for water in the design of supply systems. Yet if
anything approaching an optimum investment is to be made,
then the nature of the demand function must be understood.
Building large urban water supply systems without such consideration can only lead to misallocation of resources.

The Position of Water Supply
in Economic Development
    This study does not question the accepted position of public
water supply systems as an important element in the social
overhead facilities necessary to support economic and social
progress. It is, rather, an attempt to define more precisely
the nature of the part that public water supply systems can play
in economic development.
    The major impact of water supply in the development pro-
cess is the affect of safe and reliable sources of water on public
health. The provision of a safe source of water for domestic
consumption undeniably leads to the lessening and even eradication of waterborne disease. High rates of incidence of waterborne diseases are a major problem in most underdeveloped
countries and there has been a tendency for the occurrence of
these diseases to rise with higher rates of urbanization.
    The awareness of the nature of the relationship between
water supply and a number of serious diseases has provoked

119

much concern about the need for water supply systems. Consequently, the construction and operation of water supply systems has become a significant part of economic aid programmes. The discussion of the role of the water supply system in the development process has tended to be focused on the question of the presence or absence of water supply alone. There has been only a very limited attempt to define the optimum position of water supply systems in the overall process of economic growth.

The evidence that has been examined suggests that, apart from the contribution to public health, the provision of public water supplies is not critical to the development process. There is a need to reappraise the role of the water supply compared with alternative investments in social overhead capital and also with investment in more directly productive activities. It is unlikely that an improvement in the quality of the water used for domestic consumption would, by itself, radically improve the efficiency of the working force. Reduction in the incidence of waterborne disease will not necessarily be complete after the building of a water supply system. Yet such an effect appears to be the major underlying assumption behind the arguments advanced to support the putting of material and technical resources into urban water supply systems.

It has proved difficult to assess the concrete contributions of investment in public water supply compared to other choices for resources. The benefits to be gained from improving water supply systems are very difficult to measure; increases in productivity are not easy to define realistically. The criteria used to establish the needed capacity of a system have been drawn largely from western experience. The contemporary city in an underdeveloped country is compared to its western counterpart of the nineteenth century. But conditions in the cities of the underdeveloped countries, apart from the high incidence of disease, are not really comparable to the situation found in the western city of the late nineteenth century. The solution to the dilemma of finding the optimum level of investment in a water supply system lies in understanding the composition of the demand function for water consumed for domestic use. Only if the constituent elements of the demand for water can be understood, or the relationship between the demand for water and the level of the living environment known, can a successful attempt be made to ensure that the level of investment in water supply approaches the optimum consistent with the achievement of economic growth. The per capita supply figure used in the design of the system must be related to the actual demands likely to be achieved if it is to be meaningful. An optimum solution to the water supply problem cannot be achieved by the use of average demand figures and population projections. Generalizing demand can only lead to overinvestment in the water supply system and to the overestimation of the contributions of water supply to economic development.

The Demand for Domestic Water Supply

The case studies were structured to enquire into the nature of the demand function for domestic water supply. The consumption of water varies among the three studies, but there are significant similarities shown by the analysis, even between the areas with metered house connections and the bustees dependent upon sources of supply outside the house. The nature of the case studies is not such as to lend itself to a quantitative statement of the relationships between demand and household characteristics. They do show, however, that the demand for water, as far as this is expressed in actual consumption figures, is closely related to housing conditions and income, as well as to the possession of a house water connection and a range of plumbing facilities.

The demand for domestic water supply is a function of accessibility to water, housing conditions, the level of income, and water-using habits. Accessibility to water appears to be the most significant factor in the level of water consumption. This conclusion is supported by the large upward shift in the consumption of water between the bustee households and the households with individual connections in Kalyani and New Delhi. There is, however, a remaining large range in the per capita level of consumption within the two basic groups of households. The demand for water is not constant even within households living in dwellings with a kitchen, bathroom, and a flush toilet. The quality of housing is the most important determinant of the level of water consumption after accessibility. It seems reasonable to assume that the quality of housing or the living environment is shown by the number of persons in a household or

121

the density of occupance. The mutiple correlation analysis
shows that this is the most important single factor related to
the level of per capita consumption in Kalyani, New Delhi, and
in the bustees   This relationship between the level of water
consumption and living conditions suggests that a large increase
in water consumption can only be expected with a general improvement in the living environment.

The improvement of living conditions is a convincing explanation of the rapid expansion of water consumption in the
west. The provision of urban water supply systems coincided
with a general improvement in the level of living in the industrialized societies of the west in the late nineteenth century.
A similar increase in levels of living is not in the immediate
offing in most underdeveloped countries. Lower per capita
levels of supply can be accepted until the general level of welfare of the population increases.

The evidence from the case studies also suggests that there
would be considerable spatial differences in the demand for water, corresponding to the variation in residential conditions
within the urban area. In New Delhi the average per capita demand varies from 13.8 to 96.0 gallons between different parts
of the city and the range would be greater if poorer quality
housing had been included. A similar tendency can be seen in
Kalyani and to a lesser extent among the bustee households.
The existence of such a spatial variation in demand undermines
the wisdom of assuming that all households in the city will show
a similar level of demand for water. The use of a single mean
consumption figure does not allow the design of the water supply
system to reflect the actual residential structure of the city.

The majority of the urban population in cities such as
Calcutta are likely to be at the lower end of the demand scale
for domestic water supply. The use of a mean consumption
figure could lead to considerable overinvestment in the water
supply distribution system and the overall size of the water
works. It bears reiteration that an oversupply of water is a
misuse of resources, whatever the value of an ample water
supply as a public health measure.

There has been a tendency discernible in the provision of
social overhead facilities in underdeveloped countries to adopt
standards far above that of the capacity of the society to support. The decision to invest in social overhead projects is

taken largely outside the market framework. It is generally a
public policy decision and one in which policy makers are very
susceptible to outside influences, particularly from aid groups
whose recommendations are based upon western experience.
There is a tendency to transplant western standards rather than
to modify them to suit the particular conditions of the underdeveloped society. [1]

An example of the problems stemming from the too ready
application of western standards to the underdeveloped society
is examined by Prakash in the building of new towns in India. [2]
The standards adopted in the design of new towns in India have
led to the necessity for a very large scale subsidy of the population living in the towns, in order to keep the level of rents
within a range that the population can afford to pay. The average amount of subsidy per family per month ranged from
35.50 rupees ($4.74) to. 69.50 rupees ($9.30). In all the towns
the amount of subsidy increased with higher levels of income. [3]

Similar problems have been noted in many urban water
supply schemes and many schemes are dependent upon some
means of subsidy, ranging from the granting of soft loans to
actual subsidy of the final cost of the water supplied to the household. The decision to subsidize standards adopted in the provision of social overhead facilities is difficult to justify unless
it is assumed that urban levels of living must receive a very
high priority in the needs of the underdeveloped countries. The
real need or demand for urban water supply can be met without
the necessity to resort to subsidy.

Implications for Water Supply Policy

The empirical studies of water consumption and use in the
Calcutta Metropolitan District and New Delhi have produced
findings which are of consequence for water supply policy. It
would be rash to conclude on the basis of these studies alone

---

[1] A somewhat strong attack on this approach is made by Paul E. Koefod, "Some General Problems of Economic Development, " Land Economics, XLII, No. 3 (August,
1966), 247-259.

[2] Ved Prakash, "Financing New Towns in India" (unpublished Ph.D. dissertation,
Graduate School of Business and Public Administration, Cornell University, 1966).
See especially pp. 287-291.

[3] Ibid., p. 288.

that substantive policy changes are required. The findings do suggest, however, that when taken with other evidence, there are important questions which need to be further examined if investment in public water supply systems is to play an effective role in the process of economic development.

A number of major conclusions drawn from this study raise questions as to the wisdom of present policy. The first arises out of the observed distribution of levels of per capita water consumption and the reasons underlying this distribution. The three studies each show a similar distribution of consumption: the clustering of the majority of the households close to and below the mean but with a long tail of a few households with a very high consumption of water. The mean tends, therefore, to be highly biased by the small minority of households with very high levels of consumption, particularly in Kalyani and New Delhi. The median level of consumption is much lower than that normally used in the designing of supply systems, although all households in both areas possessed a separate bathroom and a flush toilet. Such levels of consumption do not support the fears that unless the supply is controlled, people will consume very large amounts of water. The variations in consumption that exist do not appear to be produced by the price charged for the water but by the ability of the household to use water. Related to the pattern of consumption is the close connection observed between the level of consumption and housing conditions. It suggests that if water supply is planned in isolation from the wider effort to raise the level of urban living conditions, then serious benefit allocation problems will arise. The raising of these living conditions is tied very closely to the progress in overall economic development. The existing low level of urban living conditions is a reflection of the economic poverty of the society. The dramatic repercussion of the low levels of living shown in the widespread occurrence of certain diseases may have to be accepted until the productive level of the economy is raised. In most underdeveloped societies there is a considerable disparity between urban and rural levels of living, and it has been increasingly realized in Indian planning that there is a necessity to place a higher priority on improving agricultural productivity than has been the policy under the first three five-year plans.

Specifically in the planning of water supply systems, the emphasis should be placed on meeting the existing unfilled demand (that is, supplying the unserved population), rather than in attempting to raise the levels of supply to the whole population. The existing tendency in planning water supply systems is the reverse of this. Standards are rather arbitrarily set, based upon western experience, and the systems designed around these standards. In the Master Plan for Water Supply, Sewerage and Drainage in Calcutta, for example, the adoption of two levels of demand can be traced to the exigencies of supply rather than to any attempt to allow for differential demand, with the exception of the levels adopted for Calcutta and Howrah. The two levels of supply adopted for the first phase of the project are 40 gallons per capita per day and 20 gallons per capita per day. The lower levels of demand are ascribed to those parts of the metropolitan area supplied with water from ground water sources.[4] The town of Barasat, for example, is given a demand rate of 20 gallons, although it has one of the lowest proportions of single room dwellings in the Calcutta Metropolitan District, 57.2 per cent, while Garden Reach where 81.7 per cent of the dwellings have only a single room, is given a demand rate of 40 gallons. Basing the demand levels on the supply potential alone is not likely to assure the accuracy of estimated demands!

The skewed distribution of the per capita levels of consumption also has relevance in the adoption of pricing systems for public water supply. The skewed distribution of consumption would allow for a greater flexibility in the pricing of water and supports the argument for a discriminatory tariff for domestic water supply. Any consideration of a direct pricing policy for water supply raises the problem of metering. The use of meters raises the costs of the supply system in the short run. The justification of metering is outside the purview of this study. The large range of levels of consumption between households and the association of high levels of consumption with high incomes does, however, suggest the feasibility of operating the

---

[4]Calcutta Metropolitan Planning Organization, Survey of Water Supply Resources of Greater Calcutta, Master Plan for Water Supply, Sewerage and Drainage, Calcutta Metropolitan Districts, 1966-2001, I, chap. iv.

supply system with increasing prices for higher levels of consumption of water.

Despite the contribution of water supply towards the lessening of the occurrence of certain diseases there is little reason to supply water free of charge. It is doubtful that any satisfactory system of charging can be devised for public outlets, but the provision of individual house connections should be accompanied by the introduction of a direct pricing policy.

The importance of income and living conditions in determining water consumption accords with the hypothesis that the need for domestic water supply varies with the level of economic development. It suggests that the planning of water supply systems should stress the need to ensure the widest coverage of the population, rather than raising the per capita level of consumption. It supports the contentions behind the theoretical curve for the provision of urban water supplies.

The needs for improved water supplies in the underdeveloped countries are undeniably important. The level of occurrence of certain diseases is a serious problem, and the steady recurrence of epidemics in many large urban areas is a constant reminder of the costs of insanitary and congested living conditions. Although the ultimate major cause of these diseases undoubtedly lies in the use of contaminated water for domestic purposes, the solution does not lie only in the provision of expanded or new water systems. Too often the congested urban agglomerations are already the wealthiest sections of the population and despite the dramatic death toll from cholera and other diseases, the investment of resources in urban water supplies should not be taken out of the framework of economic analysis. Waterborne diseases are not the only restraints on the quality of life in an underdeveloped country.

The benefits from improvements in water supply are not necessarily equally distributed among the population. The greatest benefits tend to go to those sections of the population with the greatest ability to use water. Ability to use water is significantly related to living conditions. If water supply is to make a direct contribution to the process of economic development, then questions of the impact of improvements are very important.

It is suggested here that there is a strong possibility of overinvestment in water supply unless the demand for water is given a more important place in the planning of water supply systems. A lower level of provision of water supply could lead to a higher level of total welfare. The contribution to welfare is dependent upon the allocation of benefits and not the provision of water alone.

The economic benefits to be expected from improvements in the supply of domestic water have not been fully investigated. Such research as has been made, and the pattern of water use and consumption shown in this study, suggests that the scale of benefits are lower than that commonly accepted in the literature. It is not feasible to make a direct inference from economic benefits to the effects of improved supply on total welfare. But it has been generally presumed that

> when we have ascertained the effect of any cause
> on economic welfare, we may, unless, of course,
> there is specific evidence to the contrary, regard
> this effect as probably equivalent in direction,
> though not in magnitude, to the effect on total wel-
> fare. [5]

The nature of the demand function for water and its intimate connection with living conditions and income does not supply any evidence to support the exemption of investment in water supply from meeting the requirements necessary for alternative investments of resources.

---

[5]A. C. Pigou, The Economics of Welfare, p. 20.

WATER SUPPLY QUESTIONNAIRES

I. KALYANI

1. Should water be provided free of charge?

2. Should water be paid for by
   a fixed fee or rate?
   taxation?
   amount used?

3. Are water meters a good idea?

4. If people do not pay their water bills should the water supply be turned off?

5. How many taps do you have?

6. Do you have
   a sink?   a shower?
   a washbasin?   a water heater?
   a bath tub?

7. How many of your taps are leaking?

8. How long have they been leaking?

9. When you have a leaking tap do you
   let it run?   tell the water supply authority?
   have a plumber repair it?   repair it yourself?

10. Do you use a dhobi?

11. Does your dhobi take clothes away to wash?

12. Do you wash clothes in the house?

13. How often do you bathe in the summer? In the winter?

14. Do you water your garden?

15. Do you use a hose to water your garden?

16. How many rooms do you have?

17. How many people live in your house?

18. How many servants do you employ?

19. How many servants live in the house?

20. What is your highest educational attainment
    Primary school?   College or University?
    Secondary school?

21. What is your occupation? (Please specify)

22. In which of the following groups does the family income fall (including Dearness Allowance and rent allowance)?

    less than 200 Rs. per month   700 - 1,000 Rs. per month
    200 - 400 Rs. per month   over 1,000 Rs. per month
    400 - 700 Rs. per month

23. How long have you been living in this house?

24. To which religious group do you belong?
    Hindu?   Christian?
    Moslem?   Sikh?

25. Do you have
    a car?   an airconditioner?
    a refrigerator?   a fan?

II. NEW DELHI

1. Should water be provided free of charge?

2. Should water be paid for by
    a fixed fee or rate?
    taxation?
    amount used?

3. Are water meters a good idea?

4. If people do not pay their water bills should the water supply be turned off?

5. Which one of the following pairs of sentences do you most agree with?
    a. (1) Everybody has a right to enough water in the same way as the air we breathe.
       (2) Water is a commodity like electricity and gas.

    b. (1) Everybody should pay the same for water.
       (2) Water should be provided free or at very low cost to poor people.

    c. (1) Water is essential for life and must be available in abundance.
       (2) Water is only one among many things needed to live comfortably.

6. Do you get enough water every day?

7. Is the water you get good water? If not, why not?

8. Do you have a storage tank for water? If yes, do you ever empty it?

9. How many taps do you have?

10. Do you have
    a sink?   a shower?
    a washbasin?   a water heater?
    a bath tub?

11. How many of your taps are leaking?

12. How long have they been leaking?

13. When you have a leaking tap do you
    let it run?
    have a plumber repair it?
    repair it yourself?

14. Do you use a dhobi?

15. Does your dhobi take clothes away to wash?

16. Do you wash clothes in the house?

130

17. How often do you bathe in the summer? In the winter?

18. Do you water your garden?

19. Do you use a hose to water your garden?

20. How many rooms do you have?

21. Do you have a separate kitchen?

22. Do you have a separate bathroom?

23. How many people live in your house (excluding servants)?

24. How many servants do you employ?

25. How many servants live in the house?

26. What is your highest educational attainment?
    None?   Secondary school?
    Primary school? College or University?

27. What is your occupation?

28. In which of the following groups does the family income fall (including Dearness Allowance and rent allowance)?
    less than 100 Rs. per month 401 - 700 Rs. per month
    101 - 200 Rs. per month   701 - 1,000 Rs. per month
    201 - 400 Rs. per month   over 1,000 Rs. per month

29. How long have you been living in this house?

30. a. Do you own or rent a house?
    b. How much rent a month do you pay?

31. In which state were you born?

32. To which religious group do you belong?
    Hindu?   Christian?
    Moslem? Sikh?
    Buddhist? Parsee?

33. Do you have
    a car/motor cycle? a radio?
    a refrigerator?   a fan?

III. CALCUTTA BUSTEES

1. Which improvement would you most prefer?
    Better street lighting Better sanitation facilities
    House tap for water   Electricity
    Better drainage

2. Do you think water should be provided free of charge?

3. Would you prefer to have your own tap and pay for water? (Cost of water should be about one rupee a month.)

4. Do you ever get involved in arguments over water?

5. Which one of each of the following pairs of sentences do you most agree with?
    a. (1) Everybody has a right to enough water in the same way as to the air we breathe.
       (2) Water is a commodity like electricity and gas.
    b. (1) Water should be paid for according to the amount used.
       (2) Water should be provided free of charge.
    c. (1) Everybody should pay the same for water.
       (2) Water should be provided free or at very low cost to poor people.

131

6. Who is responsible for providing water here?

7. To whom do you complain if the pump or standpipe is not working?

8. Do you go to the nearest public (standpipe/pump) water source? If not, why not?

9. If your pump or standpipe is not in working order where do you, or would you go for water?

10. Do you always go to the same pump or standpipe?

11. What is the water like you get from the standpipe?

12. What is the water like you get from the pump?

13. What is the unfiltered water like?

14. What is the Ganges water like?

15. Which water do you prefer to use for the following purposes? (Rank them 1-5)

	Cooking/Drinking	Washing Clothes	Bathing
Standpipe			
Pump			
Unfiltered Water			

16. What are the advantages of the water source you have marked first for
    a. Cooking/Drinking
    b. Washing Clothes
    c. Bathing

17. If you don't use your first preference, why not?

18. For what purpose do you use water from the following sources:

	Cooking/ Drinking	Washing Clothes	Washing Dishes	Bathing	Washing Cattle	*Paces— Distance from House
Standpipe						
Pump						
Unfiltered Water						

   *It will be necessary to pace the distance from each house to each water source.

19. a. Have you had any illness which you think was due to the water you used?
    b. From where did you get the water?

20. How many times did someone in your household fetch water yesterday?

		Vessel Used		
	No. Times	Circumference	Height	*Shape
Neighbour's tap				
Pump				
Standpipe				
Unfiltered Hydrant				

   *Shape: define as round jar (1)
                    cylindrical jar (2)
                    cylindrical oil can (3)
                    square oil can (4)
                    bucket (5)

21. How often do you bathe in the summer? In the winter?

22. Where do you bathe?

23. Where does the rest of the family bathe?

24. Do you use a dhobi?

25. Do you wash clothes at home?

26. a. Did you have to queue for water yesterday?
    b. How many times did you queue?
    c. For how long did you have to wait?

27. a. Do you ever buy water?
    b. How often do you buy water?
    c. How much do you pay?

28. Does the Calcutta Corporation ever distribute water by tank lorry here?

29. Are there any communal water facilities here? Do you use them?
    Toilets   Clothes washing places
    Bathing platforms   If not used, why not?

30. a. Do you keep any cattle? Cows? Water Buffalo?
    b. Where do you get water for them?
    c. Do you wash your cattle?
    d. How often?

31. a. How many rooms do you have?
    b. Is the house kutcha or pukka?

32. How many people live in your house?

33. Can you read? Bengali? Hindi? English?

34. What is your highest educational attainment?
    None?   Secondary School?
    Primary School?   College or University?

35. What is your occupation?

36. In which of the following groups does the family monthly income fall?
    less than 50 Rs. per month   201 - 250 Rs. per month
       51 - 100 Rs. per month   251 - 500 Rs. per month
      101 - 150 Rs. per month   over 500 Rs. per month
      151 - 200 Rs. per month

37. a. Do you own or rent a house?
    b. How much rent a month do you pay?

38. a. How long have you lived in this house?
    b. How long have you lived in Calcutta?

39. In which state were you born?

40. To which religious group do you belong?
    Hindu   Sikh
    Moslem   Other
    Christian

CORRELATION MATRICES

	1 Number of Taps	2 Possession of Washbasin	3 Use of Dhobi	4 No. Baths Winter	5 Number of Rooms	6 Size of Household	7 Number of Servants	8 Income	9 Possession of Refrigerator	10 Water Use Log.
1	1.00000									
2	0.86019	1.00000								
3	0.78094	0.55962	1.00000							
4	0.51366	0.50952	0.20868	1.00000						
5	0.88107	0.71076	0.78949	0.30289	1.00000					
6	-0.50195	-0.55991	0.02707	-0.47992	-0.48485	1.00000				
7	0.91434	0.76086	0.66969	0.57064	0.89709	-0.57360	1.00000			
8	0.91294	0.78729	0.81154	0.44846	0.88852	-0.40266	0.83968	1.00000		
9	0.90762	0.84786	0.54113	0.42600	0.80819	-0.72453	0.86598	0.81573	1.00000	
10	0.95877	0.76285	0.81399	0.57194	0.92470	-0.48386	0.95098	0.91872	0.83136	1.00000

New Delhi Correlation Matrix
Data Aggregated by Subdivision

	1 Number of Taps	2 Possession of Washbasin	3 Possession of Shower	4 Use of Dhobi	5 No. Baths Winter	6 No. Baths Summer	7 Number of Rooms	8 Size of Household	9 No. Servants	10 No. Servants Living in	11 Income
1	1.00000										
2	0.49193	1.00000									
3	0.48354	0.92304	1.00000								
4	0.04626	-0.04355	-0.00518	1.00000							
5	0.00841	0.00261	-0.02000	-0.01119	1.00000						
6	0.18597	0.10445	0.10545	-0.09280	0.33609	1.00000					
7	0.64177	0.39281	0.41803	0.11998	-0.03051	0.09722	1.00000				
8	0.25588	0.24202	0.22239	0.08281	-0.02165	-0.04054	0.26739	1.00000			
9	0.46490	0.32133	0.35697	0.31161	0.03227	0.12512	0.47239	0.11979	1.00000		
10	0.43594	0.31091	0.35483	0.14831	0.07165	0.26485	0.38270	0.07569	0.66872	1.00000	
11	0.38193	0.13589	0.19629	0.28796	0.03304	0.06795	0.41802	0.15116	0.59412	0.53050	1.00000
12	0.37057	0.37009	0.34832	0.02936	0.01439	0.15891	0.24476	0.03139	0.36853	0.31495	0.39811
13	0.36700	0.49959	0.50216	0.09776	-0.02679	0.15410	0.40376	0.07270	0.44221	0.33321	0.41863
14	0.12409	-0.07134	-0.00691	-0.02500	-0.16891	0.17564	0.08905	-0.43590	0.15338	0.12091	0.08063

Kalyani Correlation Matrix

12 Car Owner	13 Possession of Refrigerator	14 Water Use Log

1.00000

0.69364   1.00000

0.08029   0.13596   1.00000

	1 Number of Taps	2 Possession of Washbasin	3 Possession of Shower	4 Use of Dhobi	5 No. of baths in Winter	6 Garden Watering	7 Use of Hose	8 Number of Rooms	9 Size of Household	10 Number of Servants
1	1.00000									
2	0.65306	1.00000								
3	0.22115	0.159R2	1.00000							
4	0.35169	0.24730	0.24473	1.00000						
5	0.03364	0.06752	0.12805	0.10966	1.00000					
6	0.40269	0.40483	0.05586	0.18374	0.11695	1.00000				
7	0.57588	0.51728	0.07463	0.28737	0.09423	0.70135	1.00000			
8	0.69668	0.57362	0.16017	0.25224	0.08374	0.38538	0.58869	1.00000		
9	-0.17591	-0.23835	0.10977	-0.18080	-0.01174	-0.14322	-0.29318	-0.23022	1.00000	
10	0.61703	0.54514	0.18703	0.36461	0.17274	0.35225	0.55639	0.69720	-0.33890	1.00000
11	0.60397	0.65554	0.40013	0.36078	0.15001	0.34556	0.54320	0.62694	-0.23677	0.66854
12	0.66359	0.61647	0.11275	0.22320	0.02002	0.41571	0.60663	0.70462	-0.32507	0.60510
13	0.19166	0.11476	0.52525	0.22842	0.02957	0.07225	0.08825	0.10315	0.08531	0.10636
14	0.54334	0.54175	0.17075	0.37370	0.20508	0.36519	0.55682	0.62666	-0.45196	0.64574

New Delhi Households Correlation Matrix

	1 No. Trips Standpipe	2 No. Trips Pump	3 No. Trips U.P.H.	4 No. Baths Winter	5 Bathing at Home	6 Dhobi	7 Laundry at Home	8 Queue	9 Buy Water	10 Keeping Cattle	11 No. Cows
1	1.00000										
2	-0.27630	1.00000									
3	-0.06440	0.20882	1.00000								
4	0.04699	-0.03050	-0.02364	1.00000							
5	0.03142	0.19641	0.09398	0.10488	1.00000						
6	-0.16495	0.08522	-0.01372	-0.20876	-0.03309	1.00000					
7	0.06228	0.07595	-0.04283	0.11484	0.04312	0.04496	1.00000				
8	-0.11053	-0.15320	-0.05995	-0.24058	-0.18673	0.57777	0.09196	1.00000			
9	0.04849	0.12568	0.18143	0.02347	-0.08863	0.14663	0.03975	0.05261	1.00000		
10	-0.02040	0.26418	0.24689	-0.03640	0.01261	-0.04692	0.01997	-0.04047	0.02872	1.00000	
11	0.04592	0.28453	0.62346	-0.02963	0.04796	-0.06049	0.01625	-0.05768	0.13350	0.53726	1.00000
12	0.44578	0.06417	0.00488	-0.00453	0.07918	0.09265	-0.03910	0.01065	0.03367	0.08223	0.00786
13	0.19749	0.04060	0.00770	-0.08124	0.01451	-0.00648	0.00387	-0.07360	0.09287	-0.01962	-0.04916
14	0.22056	0.05689	-0.00159	0.26061	0.25475	-0.14709	0.09395	-0.36071	0.08964	-0.05396	-0.01293
15	-0.09593	0.04847	-0.06028	-0.04133	0.01814	0.12715	-0.04868	0.01528	-0.09625	0.12967	-0.04538
16	-0.02295	-0.05516	-0.02011	-0.05765	-0.14649	0.13267	0.03162	0.08037	0.07021	-0.03098	-0.02521
17	0.10108	0.09265	-0.02716	0.18376	0.22521	0.07675	0.06123	-0.21639	-0.01655	0.04314	0.00290
18	-0.09435	-0.18118	-0.08290	-0.12365	-0.08560	0.15828	-0.11798	0.28136	0.03985	-0.11556	-0.09404
19	0.17853	0.46737	0.16035	0.02511	0.16663	0.06816	0.12322	-0.04918	0.06354	0.14001	0.19065
20	0.28507	-0.45701	0.08907	-0.00856	-0.16558	-0.09692	-0.08600	0.10351	0.03151	-0.09338	-0.10334
21	-0.33821	0.64062	0.01718	-0.13469	0.09391	0.17018	0.03586	-0.02843	-0.00388	0.03406	0.04825

Calcutta Bustees Correlation Matrix

11 Income	12 Possession of Refrigerator	13 Possession of Fan	14 Water Use Log.
1.00000			
0.63121	1.00000		
0.23030	0.08096	1.00000	
0.62683	0.60452	0.17152	1.00000

12 Kutcha/Pukka House	13 No. People	14 Read Bengali	15 Read Hindi	16 Read Other Language	17 Level of Education	18 Religion	19 Water Use Log.	20 Distance to Standpipe Log.	21 Distance to Pump Log.
1.00000									
-0.03446	1.00000								
0.15112	0.03674	1.00000							
0.08346	-0.01776	-0.08787	1.00000						
-0.08637	0.16081	-0.14574	-0.03861	1.00000					
0.23672	0.05889	0.56209	0.40453	0.11412	1.00000				
-0.01806	0.05677	-0.40502	-0.00662	0.14372	-0.21129	1.00000			
0.04924	-0.44569	0.07567	-0.04775	-0.15071	0.05775	-0.10687	1.00000		
-0.05770	-0.07154	-0.04474	-0.04914	0.08859	-0.10921	0.16023	-0.13832	1.00000	
0.04538	-0.03183	-0.08255	0.11600	-0.03186	0.02936	-0.04845	0.28039	-0.48724	1.00000

BIBLIOGRAPHY

Abou-Garceb, A. H. "A Comparative Cholera Study between Bustee Areas of Wards 14 and 18 in the Calcutta City." Calcutta Medical Journal, LVII (April, 1960), 116-126.

--------. "Cholera in Calcutta during the Season of Prevalence, 1959." Journal of Tropical Medicine and Hygicne (May, 1960), 122-128.

--------. "Trends of Mortality from Cholera in Calcutta City Wards during Study Period of 21 Years." Calcutta Medical Journal, LVII, No. 2 (June, 1960), 181-188.

"The Detection of Cholera Endemic Centres in Calcutta City." Ibid., No. 3 (October, 1960), 343-353.

--------. "The Detection of Cholera Vibrios in Calcutta Waters: The River Hooghly and Canals." Journal of Hygiene (Cambridge), LVIII (1960), 21-33.

--------. "The Detection of Cholera Vibrios in Calcutta Waters: The Tanks and Dhobas." Internationales Journal für Prophylaktische Medezin und Sozialhygiene, VI, No. 3 (June, 1962), 64-66.

American Water Works Association, Staff Report. "A Survey of Operating Data for Water Works in 1955." Journal of the American Water Works Association, XLIX, No. 5 (May, 1955), 553-696.

Atkins, Charles H. "Some Economic Aspects of Sanitation Programs in Rural Areas and Small Towns." Paper presented to the Expert Committee on Environmental Sanitation, World Health Organization, Geneva, July 27-31, 1953, 15 pp. (Mimeographed.)

Bahamonde, O. "The Preparation of Preliminary and Complete Projects for Water Supplies," in Pan-American Health Organization, Proceedings of Seminar on Water System Design, Buenos Aires, September 20-29, 1962. (Mimeographed.)

--------. "Estudio de Tarifas de Abastecimento de Agua." Report to the Pan-American Health Organization, 1966. (Mimeographed.)

Bangalore. Administrative Report for the Year, 1962-1963, Part I. Bangalore: Corporation of the City of Bangalore, 1963, 231 pp.

Bartholomew, Harland, and Associates. See under Harland Bartholomew.

Baцer, Paul T., and B. S. Yamey. The Economics of Under-Developed Countries. Cambridge: Cambridge University Press, 1957, 271 pp.

Berry, Brian J. L., James W. Simmons, and Robert J. Tennant. "Urban Population Densities: Structure and Change." Geographical Review, LIII, No. 3 (July, 1963), 389-405.

139

Bhaskaran, T. R. A Decade of Research in Environmental Sanitation, 1951-1961. New Delhi: Indian Council of Medical Research, 1962, 67 pp.

Bogue, S. H. "Trends in Water Use." Journal of the American Water Works Association, LV, No. 5 (May, 1963), 548-554.

Bombay. Report on the Development Plan for Greater Bombay. Bombay: Government Central Press, 1964, 174 pp.

--------. "Bombay, Planning and Dreaming." Marg, XVIII, No. 3 (June, 1965). Special Issue.

Bonnerjee, J. Howrah Civic Companion. Howrah: Howrah Municipality, 1955, 524 pp.

Bose, Nirmal K. "Calcutta: A Premature Metropolis." Scientific American, CCXIII, No. 3 (September, 1965), 91-102.

Braibanti, Ralph, and Joseph J. Spengler, eds. Administration and Economic Development in India. Durham, N.C.: Duke University Press, 1963, 312 pp.

Brookings Institution. Development of Emerging Countries. Washington, D.C.: Brookings Institution, 1962, 239 pp.

Brush, J. E. "The Morphology of Indian Cities," in India's Urban Future. Edited by R. Turner. Bombay: Oxford University Press, Indian Branch, 1962.

Bulsara, Jal F. Problems of Rapid Urbanization in India. Bombay: Popular Prakashan, 1964, 215 pp.

Burns, Leland S. "Cost-Benefit Analysis of a Social Overhead Project for Regional Development." Papers of the Regional Science Association, XVI (1966), 155-161.

Calcutta Metropolitan Planning Organization. "Memorandum on Fourth Plan Proposals for the Development of the Calcutta Metropolitan District, " n.d., 26 pp. and appendices. (Mimeographed.)

--------. "Interim Summary Report, Survey of Water Resources of Greater Calcutta." Draft No. 1, 1964. (Mimeographed.)

--------. "Slum Improvement Scheme, Pilkhana Bustee, Howrah, " n.d. (Mimeographed.)

--------. "Survey of Water Supply Resources of Greater Calcutta." Status Report of the UN Special Fund, World Health Organization, Project India—170, March, 1965, 57 pp. and maps. (Mimeographed.)

--------. "Calcutta Metropolitan District Emergency Water Supply Scheme." Report, n.d., 6 pp. (Mimeographed.)

"A Preliminary Report on Housing Conditions and Problems in the Context of CMD Planning." Calcutta Metropolitan District Planning Team, 1965, 50 pp. (Mimeographed.)

--------. Basic Development Plan, Calcutta Metropolitan District, 1966-1986 Calcutta: CMPO, 1966, 176 pp

-------- Survey of Water Supply Resources of Greater Calcutta, Master Plan for Water Supply, Sewerage and Drainage, Calcutta Metropolitan District, 1966-2001, I, Detailed Report prepared for the World Health Organization by Metcalfe and Eddy Ltd. and Engineering Sciences Inc., August, 1966.

Camaroun, Ministère des Travaux Public et des Transports, Direction des Travaux Public. Bulletin Statistique, Production et Distribution D'Énergie Électrique et D'Eau Potable (1962-1965), annual.

Census of India. See under India.

Chakravati, D. N. Annual Report on the State of Health of West Bengal, 1959. Calcutta: Government of West Bengal, Directorate of Health Services, 1963, 668 pp.

Chatterjee, S. K., ed. The Recommendations of the West Bengal State Public Health Expert Committee on the Control and Eradication of Smallpox and Cholera, and Special Studies on the Problems. West Bengal Directorate of Health Services, Technical Memorandum No. 1. Allpore: West Bengal Government Press, 1959, 38 pp.

--------. "The Epidemiological Aspects of Cholera in Calcutta. " Indian Journal of Medical Research, LII, No 8 (August, 1964), 760-769.

Chatterjee, S. K., and A. Das Gupta. Cholera in Calcutta. West Bengal Directorate of Health Services, Technical Memorandum No. 2. Alipore: West Bengal Government Press, 1959, 67 pp.

Chatterjee, S. P. Fifty Years of Science in India: Progress of Geography. Calcutta: Indian Science Congress Association, 1963.

Coale, Ann J., and Edgar M. Hoover. Population Growth and Economic Development in Low Income Countries. Princeton: Princeton University Press, 1958, 389 pp.

Davis, K. "Urbanization in India: Past and Future, " in India's Urban Future. Edited by R. Turner. Bombay: Oxford University Press, Indian Branch, 1962.

Delhi, Development Authority. Master Plan for Delhi. Vol. II, Part III. Delhi: Delhi Development Authority, n.d.

Delhi, Municipal Committee. Annual Administration Report, 1960-1961. Delhi: Municipal Press, 1961, 391 pp.

Dhillon, H. S. "Life in a Bustee Area, " All-India Institute of Hygiene and Public Health, Calcutta, 1959, 49 pp. (Mimeographed.)

Dieterich, Bernd H., and John M. Henderson. Urban Water Supply Conditions and Needs in Seventy-Five Develop in Countries World Health Organization Public Hea Paper No. 23. Geneva: WHO, 1963, 92 pp.

Dorfman, Robert, ed. Measuring Benefits of Governmental Investments, Studies of Government Finance. Washington, D.C.: Brookings Institution, 1965, 429 pp.

Dublin, L. I., and A. J. Lotka. The Money Value of a Man. New York: Ronald Press, 1930.

Dunn, D. F., and T. E. Larson. "Relationship of Domestic Water Use to Assessed Valuation, with Selected Demographic and Socio-Economic Variables." Journal of the American Water Works Association, LV, No. 4 (April, 1963), 441-449.

Dutt, A. K., and S. K. Chakravorty. "Reality of Calcutta Conurbation." National Geographic Journal of India, IX, Parts III & IV (September and December, 1963), 161-174.

Fair, G. M., and J. C. Geyer. Water Supply and Waste-Water Disposal. New York: John Wiley, 1959, 973 pp.

Fourt, Louis. "Forecasting the Urban Residential Demand for Water." Agricultural Economics Seminar, University of Chicago, Department of Economics, February, 1958, 9 pp. (Mimeographed.)

Fox, Irving K., and Orris C. Herfindahl. "Attainment of Efficiency in Satisfying Demands for Water Resources." American Economic Review, LIV (May, 1964), 198-206.

Gadgil, D. R. Planning and Economic Policy in India. Poona: Gokhale Institute of Politics and Economics, 1965, 354 pp.

Galbraith, J. Kenneth. Economic Development in Perspective. Cambridge: Harvard University Press, 1962, 76 pp.

Ginsburg, Norton. "The Regional Concept and Planning Regions." Housing, Building and Planning, Nos. 12 & 13, Regional Planning. New York: United Nations, 1959, pp. 31-45.

--------, ed. Essays on Geography and Economic Development. Department of Geography Research Paper No. 62. Chicago: Department of Geography, Uni-versity of Chicago, 1960, 173 pp.
--------,Atlas of Economic Development. Chicago: University of Chicago Press, 1961, 119 pp.

Gist, N. P. "The Ecological Structure of An Asian City: An East-West Comparison." Population Review, II, No. 1 (January, 1958), 17-25.

Goode, S. W. Municipal Calcutta. Edinburgh: Calcutta Corporation, 1916, 410 pp.

Guba, M. "The Morphology of Calcutta." Geographical Review of India, XV, No. 3 (September, 1953), 20-28.

Guha, M., and A. B. Chatterjee. "Serampore—A Study in Urban Geography." Geographical Review of India, XVI, No. 4 (December, 1954), 38-44.

Guha, Uma. A Short Sample Survey of the Socio-Economic Conditions of Saheb-Bagan Bustee, Calcutta. Calcutta: Department of Anthropology, Indian Museum, 1958, 36 pp.

Harbeger, A. C. "Cost-Benefit Analysis and Economic Growth." The Economic Weekly (Bombay), Annual Number (February, 1962), 207-222.

Harland Bartholomew and Associates. Water and Sewerage Problems, Greater Karachi. St. Louis: Privately Printed, 1952, 177 pp.

Healey, J. M. The Development of Social Overhead Capital in India, 1950-1960. Bombay: Oxford University Press, Indian Branch, 1965, 180 pp.

Henderson, John M. "Report on the Global Urban Water Supply Program, Costs in Developing Nations, 1961-1975," International Cooperation Administration, Washington, D.C., June, 1961, 99 pp. (Mimeographed.)

Hirschmann, Albert O. The Strategy of Economic Development. New Haven: Yale University Press, 1958, 217 pp.

--------. "Obstacles to Development, A Classification and a Quasi-Vanishing Act." Economic Development and Cultural Change, XIII, No. 4, Part I (July, 1965).

Hirshliefer, Jack, James C. DeHaven, and Jerome W. Milliman. Water Supply: Economics, Technology, and Policy. Chicago: University of Chicago Press, 1960, 378 pp.

Hoselitz, Bert F. The Progress of Underdeveloped Areas. Chicago: University of Chicago Press, 1952, 297 pp.

--------. "The Cities of India and Their Problems." Annals of the Association of American Geographers, XLIX, No. 2 (June, 1959), 223-231.

Howe, Charles W., and F. P. Linaweaver, Jr. "The Impact of Price on Residential Water Demand and Its Relation to System Design and Price Structure." Water Resources Research, III, No. 1 (First Quarter, 1967), 13-32.

Hubli-Dharwar. Administrative Reports, March, 1962, and 1962-1963. Hubli: Municipal Corporation of Hubli-Dharwar, 1963, 145 pp.

India, Census of India, 1961. Vol. XVI: West Bengal and Sikkim, Part IV (1), Report and Main Tables on Housing and Establishments.

India, Committee on Plan Projects. Report on National Water Supply and Sanitation Schemes. New Delhi: Government of India Press, 1961, 74 pp.

India, Ministry of Food and Agriculture. Report of Residential Buildings. New Delhi: Government of India Press, 1961, 86 pp.

India, Ministry of Health. Report of the Environmental Hygiene Committee, October, 1949. New Delhi: Government of India Press, 1956, 208 pp.

--------. Control of Smallpox and Cholera in India. New Delhi: Government of India Press, 1959, 181 pp.

India, Ministry of Health, Committee on Public Health Engineering Manual and Code of Practice. Proceedings and Recommendations, Seminar on Financing and Management of Water and Sewerage Works. New Delhi: Government of India Press, 1964, 86 pp.

--------. Report of the National Water Supply and Sanitation Committee, 1960-1961. Simla: Government of India Press, 1962, 167 pp.

--------. Public Health Engineering Manual and Code of Practice, Section 1-A, Manual on Water Supply. New Delhi: Director-General of Health Services, 1962, 180 pp.

India, Ministry of Labour. Low-Cost Housing for Industrial Workers. New Delhi: Office of Chief Advisor of Factories, 1954, 69 pp.

143

India, National Council for Applied Economic Research. Criteria for the Fixation of Water Rates and Selection of Irrigation Projects. Bombay: Asia, 1959, 156 pp.

--------. A Strategy for the Fourth Plan. Occasional Paper No. 11. New Delhi: NCAER, 1964, 85 pp.

India, Planning Commission. Report of the Committee on Distribution of Income and Levels of Living. New Delhi: Government of India Press, 1964, 107 pp.

--------. A Report on the Implementation of the National Water Supply and Sanitation Programme. New Delhi: Government of India Press, 1965, 40 pp.

--------. Third Five Year Plan. New Delhi: Government of India Press, 1961, 774 pp.

--------. Third Five Year Plan, Progress Report, 1961-1962. New Delhi: Government of India Press, 1963.

--------. Annual Plan, 1966-1967. New Delhi: Government of India Press, 1966, 133 pp.

--------. Committee on Plan Projects, Building Projects Team. Report on Residential Buildings. New Delhi: Government of India Press, 1961.

India, Research Programmes Committee. Criteria for Appraising the Feasibility of Irrigation Projects. New Delhi: Government of India Press, 1964, 102 pp.

--------. Report on the Conservation of Water Resources and the Control of Water Pollution. New Delhi: Government of India Press, 1963, 41 pp.

Indian Council of Medical Research. Manual of Standards of Quality for Drinking Water Supplies. Special Report Series No. 44. New Delhi: Indian Council of Medical Research, 1962, 10 pp.

International Bank for Reconstruction and Development. World Bank Atlas of Per Capita Product and Population. Washington, D.C.: World Bank, 1966.

Jakobson, Leo. "A Note on Housing in the Calcutta Metropolitan District." Report to the Ford Foundation Advisory Planning Group, Calcutta Metropolitan Plan, January 15, 1965. (Mimeographed.)

Japan. Health Statistics (1962).

Johnson, Ralph W. "Water Shortages, Real and Imaginary." Address delivered to the Portland City Club, Portland, Oregon, March 12, 1965, 12 pp. (Mimeographed.)

Kally, Elisha. "Determination of Water Supply Investment Priorities in Developing Countries." Journal of the American Water Works Association, LVII, No. 8 (August, 1965), 955-964.

Kamal, A. M. "Endemicity and Epidemicity of Cholera." Bulletin of the World Health Organization, XXVIII, No. 3 (1963), 277-287.

Kelso, M. M. "Economic Analysis in the Allocation of the Federal Budget to Resource Development," in Water Resource Development. Edited by S. C. Smith and E. N. Castle. Ames: Iowa State University Press, 1964.

144

Kendrew, W. G. Climate of the Continents. Oxford: Oxford University Press, 1961.

Kindleburger, Charles P. Economic Development. New York: McGraw-Hill, 1958, 325 pp.

Koefod, Paul E. "Some General Problems of Economic Development." Land Economics, XLII, No. 3 (August, 1966), 247-259.

Krutilla, J., and O. Eckstein. Multiple Purpose River Development. Baltimore: Johns Hopkins University Press, 1958.

Kuznets, Simon. Six Lectures on Economic Growth. Glencoe, Ill.: Free Press, 1959. 122 pp.

Learmonth, A. T. A. "Retrospect on a Project in Applied Regional Geography, Mysore State, India," in Geographers and the Tropics: Liverpool Essays. Edited by R. W. Steele and R. Mansell Prothero. London: Longmans, Green, 1964, 323-348.

Lewis, John P. Quiet Crisis in India. Bombay: Asia, 1963, 350 pp.

Lewis, W. Arthur. Theory of Economic Growth. London: Unwin, 1955, 453 pp.

Linaweaver, F. P., Jr. "Report II, Phase Two, Residential Water Use Research Project," Sanitary Engineering and Water Resources, Johns Hopkins University, Baltimore, June, 1965, 62 pp. (Mimeographed.)

Linaweaver, F. P., Jr., J. C. Geyer, and J. B. Wolff. "Final and Summary Report on Phase Two of Residential Water Use Research Project," Department of Environmental Engineering Science, Johns Hopkins University, June, 1966, 95 pp. (Mimeographed.)

Logan, John. "The International Municipal Water Supply Program: A Health and Economic Appraisal." American Journal of Tropical Medicine and Hygiene, IX, No. 5 (September, 1960), 469-476.

Maas, Arthur, et al. Design of Water Resource Systems. Cambridge: Harvard University Press, 1962, 620 pp.

MacNamara, C. History of Asiatic Cholera. London: Macmillan, 1876, 476 pp.

McClelland, D. C. "Does Education Contribute to Economic Growth?" Economic Development and Cultural Change, XIV, No. 3 (April, 1963), 260-261.

McPhee, W. T. "Water Supply for Saigon." Civil Engineering, XXXV, No. 9 (September, 1965), 59-65.

Madras, Corporation of Madras. Administrative Report, 1963-64, Part 1. Main Report. Madras: Corporation of Madras, 1964, 274 pp.

Mehta, V. C. Report of the Broad Civic Survey of Cuttack. Cuttack: Government of Orissa, Town Planning Organization, 1956, 144 pp.

Meier, G. M., ed. Leading Issues in Development Economics. New York: Oxford University Press, 1964, 572 pp.

Miller, Arthur P. Water and Man's Health. U.S. State Department Agency for International Development, Community Water Supply Technical Series No. 5. Washington, D.C.: U.S. Government Printing Office, 1962, 92 pp.

145

Milliman, Jerome W. "Policy Horizons for Future Urban Water Supply." Land Economics, XLIX, No. 2 (May, 1963), 109-132.

Modern Sanitation, III, No. 10 (1951).

Murdoch, J. A. "Seventy-Five Years of Too Cheap Water—Nine Years Later." Journal of the American Water Works Association, LVII, No. 8 (August, 1965), 943-947.

Nigan, M. N. "Evolution of Lucknow." National Geographic Journal of India, VI, No. 1 (March, 1960), 30-46.

Nyerges, N. "Social and Economic Considerations Affecting the Development of Design Standards," in Pan-American Health Organization, Proceedings of Seminar on Water System Design, Buenos Aires, September 20-29, 1962. (Mimeographed.)

Okun, B., and R. W. Richardson. Studies in Economic Development. New York: Holt, Rhinehart & Winston, 1961, 49 pp.

Pan-American Health Organization. Tarifas De Aqua. Washington, D.C.: PAHO, 1961, 68 pp.

--------. "Proceedings of Seminar on Water System Design," Buenos Aires, September 20-29, 1962. (Mimeographed.)

--------. Aqua. Report of the Regional Conference on Water Supply in the Americas, Washington, D.C., October 18-20, 1965. Scientific Publication No. 132. Washington, D.C.: PAHO, 1966, 109 pp.

--------. Hechos Sobre, El Abasteciemiento de Aqua en las Americas. Regional Conference on Water Supply in the Americas, Washington, D.C., October 18-20, 1965. Washington, D. C.: PAHO, 1965, 41 pp.

--------. "Summary on the Water Supply Situation in the Eastern Caribbean," Washington, D. C., October, 1966, 26 pp. (Mimeographed.)

Patna. Administration Report of the Chief Executive Officer for Patna Municipal Corporation, 1959-1960. Patna: Patna Municipal Corporation, 1960, 49 pp.

Pigou, A.C. The Economics of Welfare. 4th edition. London: Macmillan, 1960.

Porges, R. "Factors Influencing Per Capita Water Consumption." Water and Sewage Works, CIV, No. 5 (May, 1957), 199-204.

Prakash, Ved. "Financing New Towns in India." Unpublished Ph. D. dissertation, Graduate School of Business and Public Administration, Cornell University, 1966.

Pyatt, Edwin E., and Peter P. Rogers. "On Estimating Benefit-Cost Ratios for Water Supply Investments." American Journal of Public Health, LII, No. 10 (October, 1962), 1729-1742.

Pyatt, Edwin E., Peter P. Rogers, and Hassan Sheikh. "Benefit-Cost Analysis for Municipal Water Supplies." Land Economics, XL, No. 4 (November, 1964), 444-449.

Qurashi, G. M. "Water Demand in Sweden." Journal of the American Water Works Association, LIV, No. 7 (July, 1962), 776-780.

146

--------. "Domestic Water Use in Sweden." Ibid., LV, No. 4 (April, 1963), 451-455.

Raj, K. N. Some Economic Aspects of the Bhakra Nangel Project. Bombay: Asia, 1960, 140 pp.

Rao, P. Towns of Mysore State. Bombay: Asia, 1964, 120 pp.

Rostow, Walter W. The Stages of Economic Growth. London: Cambridge University Press, 1960, 179 pp.

--------, ed. The Economics of Take-Off into Sustained Growth. London: Macmillan, 1963, 482 pp.

Sen, S. N. The City of Calcutta: A Socio-Economic Survey, 1954-55 to 1957-58. Calcutta: Bookland Private, 1960, 271 pp.

Sewell, W. R. D., J. Davis, A. D. Scott, and D. W. Ross. Guide to Benefit-Cost Analysis. Prepared for the Resources for Tomorrow Conference, Montreal, October 23-28, 1961. Ottawa: Queen's Printer, 1962, 49 pp.

Sheaffer, John R., and A. J. Zeigel. The Water Resource in Northeastern Illinois: Planning Its Use. Northeastern Illinois Planning Commission Technical Memorandum No. 4. Chicago: NIPC, 1966, 182 pp.

Siedel, H. F., and E. R. Baumann. "A Statistical Analysis of Water Works Data for 1955." Journal of the American Water Works Association, XLIX, No. 12 (December, 1957), 1531-1580.

Singh, Baljit, and Shridhar Misra. Benefit-Cost Analysis of the Sarda Canal System. Bombay: Asia, 1965, 275 pp.

Singh, M. M., and Abhijit Datta. Metropolitan Calcutta: Special Agencies for Housing, Planning, and Development. Calcutta Research Series, Occasional Reports. New York: Institute of Public Administration, 1963, 172 pp.

Singh, R. L. Bangalore: An Urban Survey. Varanasi: National Geographical Society of India, 1964, 165 pp.

Singh, Ujagir. Allahabad: A Study in Urban Geography. Varanasi: National Geographical Society of India, 1961, 183 pp.

Steele, R. W., and R. Mansell Prothero, eds. See under Learmonth.

Smith, Stephen C., and Emery N. Castle, eds. Water Resource Development: Economics and Public Policy. Ames: Iowa State University Press, 1964, 463 pp.

Sovani, N. V. "The Analysis of 'Over-Urbanization.'" Economic Development and Cultural Change, XII, No. 2 (January, 1964), 113-122.

Taylor, Carl C., et al. India's Roots of Democracy. Calcutta: Orient Longmans, 1965, 694 pp.

The Statesman (Calcutta), June 9, 1966.

Tinbergen, Jan. The Design of Development. Baltimore: Johns Hopkins University Press, 1958, 99 pp.

--------. Central Planning. New Haven: Yale University Press, 1964, 150 pp.

Turner, Roy, ed. India's Urban Future. Bombay: Oxford University Press, Indian Branch, 1962, 470 pp.

Twort, A. C. A Textbook of Water Supply. London: Edward Arnold, 1963, 422 pp.

Tyrwhitt, Jacqueline, ed. Patrick Geddes in India. London: Lund Humphries, 1947, 103 pp.

United Kingdom, Central Advisory Water Committee. Sub-Committee on the Growing Demand for Water, Final Report. London: HMSO, 1962, 43 pp.

United Nations. Proceedings of the Fifth Regional Conference on Water Resources Development in Asia and the Far East. Water Resource Series No. 23. New York: UN, 1963, 208 pp.

--------. Water Desalination in Developing Countries. New York: UN, 1964, 325 pp.

--------. Processes and Problems of Industrialization in Underdeveloped Countries. New York: UN, 1955.

--------. Report on the Regional Seminar on Public Administration Problems of New and Rapidly Growing Towns in Asia. New York: UN, 1962, 90 pp.

United Nations, Department of Economic Affairs. Measures for the Economic Development of Underdeveloped Countries. New York: UN, 1951, 108 pp.

--------. Planning for Balanced Social and Economic Development. New York: UN, 1964, 281 pp.

United Nations, Research Institute for Social Development. Social and Economic Factors in Development. Report No. 3. Geneva: UN, 1965.

--------. The Level of Living Index. Report No. 4. Geneva: UN, 1966, 90 pp.

--------. "Cost-Benefit Analysis of Social Projects." Report No. 7, Geneva, April, 1966, 129 pp. (Mimeographed.)

United Nations, Statistical Office. Demographic Year Book, 1963. New York: UN, 1964.

--------. Yearbook of National Account Statistics 1963. New York: UN, 1964, 333 pp.

United States, Department of Health, Education and Welfare, Public Health Service. Economic Benefits from Public Health Services. Washington, D.C.: Office of the Surgeon-General, 1964, 31 pp.

United States, State Department, International Cooperation Administration. "Engineering Management of Water Supply Systems." Regional Seminar, Near East - South Asia, Tehran, Iran, June 17-27, 1961, 179 pp. (Mimeographed.)

--------. "Engineering Management of Water Supply Systems." Regional Seminar, Far East - Southeast Asia, Hna Hia, Thailand, July 5-14, 1961, 105 pp. (Mimeographed.)

"Report of the Panel of Expert Consultants to the International Coopera- tion Administration on the Community Water Supply Development Program," Washington, D.C., April 12-14, 1960. (Mimeographed.)

Vanes, J. A., K. E. Symons, and D. A. McTavish. "The Diverse Effects of Water Pollution on the Economy—Domestic and Municipal Water Use." Pollution and Our Environment, Background Papers, The Canadian Council of Resource Min- isters Conference, October-November, 1966, Montreal. (Mimeographed.)

Wagner, Edmund G., and J. N. Lanoix. Water Supply for Rural Areas and Small Communities. World Health Organization Monograph Series No. 42. Geneva: WHO, 1959, 340 pp.

Wagner, Edmund G., and Luis Wannoni. "Anticipated Savings in Venezuela through the Construction of Safe Water Supplies in Rural Areas." Paper presented to the Expert Committee on Environmental Sanitation, World Health Organization, Geneva, July 27-31, 1953, 13 pp. (Mimeographed.)

Warford, J. J. "Water 'Requirements': The Investment Decision in the Water Supply Industry." The Manchester School of Economic and Social Studies, XXXIV, No. 1 (January, 1966), 87-106.

West Bengal, Directorate of Health Services, Vital Statistics Division. "A Study of Cholera Endemicity in West Bengal, 1946-1960," Vital Statistics Special Report, July, 1963, 101 pp. (Mimeographed.)

West Bengal, Local Self-Government Department. Report of the Corporation of Calcutta Investigation Commission, Vol. II. Alipore: West Bengal Government Press, 1951, 534 pp.

--------. "Report of the Committee of Enquiry into the Supply of Filtered Water in Calcutta," Calcutta, August, 1965, 24 pp. (Mimeographed.)

--------. Kalyani. Alipore: West Bengal Government Press, 1958, 12 pp.

West Bengal, Local Self-Government and Panchayat Department. Report of the Corporation of Calcutta Enquiry Committee, Vol. I. Alipore: West Bengal Government Press, 1962, 39 pp.

West Bengal, State Statistical Bureau. Report of the Bustee Survey in Calcutta, 1958-1959. 17 volumes; some volumes unpublished. Alipore: West Bengal Government Press.
--------. Statistical Abstract, 1961. Alipore: West Bengal Government Press, 1965.

--------. Estimates of State Income and Its Regional Differentials. Calcutta: Director of Information, 1965.

Wiener, Aaron. Water Development Procedures in Arid and Semi-Arid Regions. Tel Aviv: Tahal, Water Planning for Israel, March, 1963, 14 pp.

--------. Development and Management of Water Supplies under Conditions of Scarcity of Water. Tel Aviv: Tahal, Water Planning for Israel, April, 1964, 13 pp.

Wiesbrod, Burton A. Economics of Public Health. Philadelphia: University of Pennsylvania Press, 1961, 127 pp.

Wolff, J. B. "Forecasting Residential Water Requirements." Journal of the American Water Works Association, XLIX, No. 3 (March, 1957), 225-235.

Wolman, Abel B. "Effects of Population Changes on Environmental Health Problems and Programs." Journal of the American Water Works Association, LVII, No. 7 (July, 1965), 811-818.

--------. "The Metabolism of Cities." Scientific American, CCXIII, No. 8 (September, 1965), 179-190.

Wolman, Abel B., and H. M. Bosch. "U.S. Water Supply Lessons Applicable to Developing Countries." Journal of the American Water Works Association, LV, No. 8 (August, 1963), 946-956.

Wolman, Abel B., et al. "Survey of Water Supply Resources of Greater Calcutta." U.N. Special Fund, World Health Organization Project India— 170, Calcutta, 1964, 240 pp. (Mimeographed.)

--------. "Assignment Report on Water Supply and Sewage Disposal, Greater Calcutta." World Health Organization Project India —170. WHO, Regional Office for Southeast Asia, New Delhi. (Mimeographed.)

Wong, Shue Tuck, John R. Sheaffer, and Harold B. Gotass. "Multivariate Statistical Analysis of Water Supplies." Paper presented at the American Society of Civil Engineers, Water Resources Engineering Conference, Milwaukee, Wisconsin, May 14, 1963, 17 pp.

World Health Organization. International Standards for Drinking Water, 2nd edition. Geneva: WHO, 1963, 206 pp.

--------. Environmental Change and Resulting Impacts on Health. Technical Report Series No. 292. Geneva: WHO, 1964, 23 pp.

--------. Environmental Health Aspects of Metropolitan Planning and Development. Technical Report Series No. 297. Geneva: WHO, 1965, 66 pp.

--------. "Proceedings and Papers of Inter-Regional Seminar on Integration of Community Water Supplies into Planning of Economic Development," Geneva, September 19-28, 1967. (Mimeographed; to be published.)

--------. U.N. Special Fund, Project India —170. See under Calcutta Metropolitan Planning Organization.

World Health Organization, Engineering Reports. "Water Supply Feasibility Study." Monrovia, Liberia, January, 1964.

--------. "Dahomey, Ville de Cotonou, Amélioration et Extension du Système D'Approvisionnement en Eau Potable." Report, July, 1965.

--------. "Engineering Study, Water Supply for Mersin," Turkey, 1965.

--------. "Master Plan for Water Supply." Government of Ghana, Engineering Report for Accra-Tema Metropolitan Area, 1965.

--------. "Report on Operation and Management of the Water Service Bureau." Special City of Seoul, Korea, 1965.

World Health Organization, Regional Office for Southeast Asia. "Community Water Supplies: The Position in the Southeast Asia Region." Working Paper No. 1, Regional Committee, Fifteenth Session, New Delhi, 1962. (Mimeographed.)

Young, Robert C. "Education Planning and Economic Criteria in India's Context." Memorandum to Ford Foundation Advisory Planning Group, Calcutta, January, 1966. (Mimeographed.)

Zaheer, M., B. G. Prasad, K. K. Govil, and T. Bhadury. "A Note on Urban Water Supply in Uttar Pradesh." Journal of the Indian Medical Association, XXXVIII, No. 4 (February 16, 1962), 177-182.

Lightning Source UK Ltd.
Milton Keynes UK
UKHW010000210722
406167UK00001B/263

9 781487 587154